How the
REFRIGERATOR
CHANGED HISTORY

How the
REFRIGERATOR
CHANGED HISTORY

by Lydia Bjornlund

CONTENT CONSULTANT

Sunil S. Mehendale, PhD

Assistant Professor

School of Technology, Michigan Technological University

ESSENTIAL LIBRARY OF
INVENTIONS

Essential Library

An Imprint of Abdo Publishing | abdopublishing.com

abdopublishing.com

Published by Abdo Publishing, a division of ABDO, PO Box 398166, Minneapolis, Minnesota 55439. Copyright © 2016 by Abdo Consulting Group, Inc. International copyrights reserved in all countries. No part of this book may be reproduced in any form without written permission from the publisher. Essential Library™ is a trademark and logo of Abdo Publishing.

Printed in the United States of America, North Mankato, Minnesota
052015
092015

Cover Photos: Tara Patta/Shutterstock Images, left; Shutterstock Images, right
Interior Photos: Hulton-Deutsch Collection/Corbis, 2, 73; iStockphoto, 6–7, 32–33, 93 (top), 98–99; The Protected Art Archive/Alamy, 9; Florida Department of Environmental Protection, 11; Mary Evans Picture Library/Alamy, 13; Public Domain, 15; J. Scott Applewhite/AP Images, 17; Tara Patta/Shutterstock Images, 19; DeAgostini/SuperStock, 20–21; Detroit Publishing Co./Library of Congress, 24; DIZ Muenchen GmbH/Sueddeutsche Zeitung Photo/Alamy, 29; Library of Congress, 31, 36; Interfoto/Alamy, 40; Red Line Editorial, 42–43; Russell Lee/FSA/OWI Collection/Library of Congress, 44–45; Bettmann/Corbis, 48, 64–65, 80; Meat and Wool New Zealand, 53; Everett Collection Inc./Alamy, 54–55; North Wind Picture Archives, 56; Gottscho-Schleisner, Inc./Library of Congress, 61; Schenectady Museum/Hall of Electrical History Foundation/Corbis, 63, 69; Jeff Morgan 06/Alamy, 71; Camerique/ClassicStock/Corbis, 74–75; Theodor Horydczak, 79; William Gottlieb/Corbis, 83; Jeremy Sutton-Hibbert/Alamy, 84–85; Brian A. Jackson/Shutterstock Images, 88; DCPhoto/Alamy, 92; Christopher Futcher/iStockphoto, 92–93; ImageBroker/Alamy, 93 (bottom); Gary Burchell/Getty Images, 97; Reimar 5/Alamy, 98

Editor: Rebecca Rowell
Series Designer: Craig Hinton

Library of Congress Control Number: 2015930955

Cataloging-in-Publication Data

Bjornlund, Lydia.
 How the refrigerator changed history / Lydia Bjornlund.
   p. cm. -- (Essential library of inventions)
 Includes bibliographical references and index.
 ISBN 978-1-62403-786-3
 1. Refrigeration and refrigeration machinery--History--Juvenile literature. 2. Inventions--Juvenile literature. I. Title.
 621.5--dc23
                                          2015930955

CONTENTS

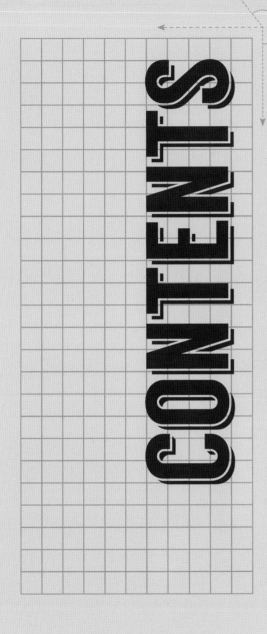

CHAPTER 1

A COOL
MIRACLE

On July 14, 1847, a group of well-heeled guests gathered to celebrate Bastille Day, a French holiday, in Apalachicola, Florida. Monsieur Rosan, the French consul, gave a toast: "On Bastille Day, France gave her citizens what they wanted; Rosan gives his guests what they want, cool wines! Even if it demands a miracle!"[1] To the surprise of those in the audience, Rosan's toast cued waiters, who arrived with trays of champagne nestled in ice. Rosan's guest, John Gorrie, had orchestrated the stunt to demonstrate the possibilities of his new ice machine.

Cooling beverages with ice cubes is a modern convenience.

THE ICE CUBE TRAY

Although it is not known for sure who invented the first ice cube tray, many historians credit Gorrie. Documents show Gorrie used his refrigeration machine to freeze ice and provided iced drinks to his patients. By the 1920s, ice cube trays often came standard with refrigerators. The basic design remained the same, but inventors experimented with different materials in search of a tray that would provide the flexibility needed to allow users to twist the tray and pop out the ice. The first patents were for a rubber tray. By 1933, stainless steel trays were popular. By the 1950s and 1960s, the plastic tray emerged and is common today.

Gorrie, a local physician-turned-inventor, had not created his ice maker to cool drinks for the wealthy. Rather, he wanted it to prevent yellow fever, which had hit Apalachicola in 1841. Doctors had not yet discovered that yellow fever and malaria, as well as other tropical diseases, were spread by mosquitoes. They believed warm air caused the diseases. Gorrie noticed the fevers caused by these maladies stopped in cold weather. To contain the spread of the disease and ease the suffering of patients, Gorrie suspended a bucket of ice from the infirmary's ceiling. Because cool air is heavier than warm air, it drops lower than warm air, pushing the warm air above it. As a result, placing the bucket near the ceiling helped to cool the room. Some researchers say Gorrie added a fan to speed up the cooling process, but no one is sure how he would have been able to add a fan.

Ice was essential to this early air conditioning system. But finding ice was no easy feat. Most of the ice available in the southern United States

People in southern states relied on the work of ice harvesters in colder climates.

came from New York and New England, where workers harvested it in the winter from frozen rivers and ponds. In winter, ice was expensive. In summer, it was often completely unavailable.

When Gorrie heard about other scientists' experiments with mechanical ice systems, he quit his job as a physician and threw himself into creating an ice-making machine. In an 1844 article in Apalachicola's *Commercial Advertiser* newspaper, Gorrie described how his invention would work:

> *If the air were highly compressed, it would heat up by the energy of compression. If this compressed air were run through metal pipes cooled with water, and if this air cooled to the water temperature was expanded down to atmospheric pressure again, very low temperatures could be obtained, even low enough to freeze water in pans in a refrigerator box.*[2]

Gorrie recognized that his invention would be far easier to sell if it appealed to an audience beyond patients suffering from malaria and their doctors. He wrote about the benefits of artificial ice, promoting its commercial and humanitarian benefits. Gorrie found a wealthy investor to sponsor his project and enlisted the Cincinnati Iron Works to build a model of this first commercially available refrigeration machine.

A replica of John Gorrie's ice machine is on display in the Gorrie Museum in Apalachicola, Florida.

A Century in the Making

Gorrie's design was based on principles established by William Cullen of the University of Glasgow, in Scotland, almost a century earlier. Cullen showed that when a liquid evaporates, it extracts heat from its surroundings. Compressing a gas, on the other hand, causes it to heat up. Removing the pressure causes the gas to expand and absorb heat. In 1755, Cullen demonstrated this principle to create a small amount of ice by heating ether, a flammable liquid, until it became a gas. This principle of refrigeration—cooling caused by the rapid expansion of gases—remains basic to refrigeration today.

In 1805, the American inventor Oliver Evans capitalized on Cullen's

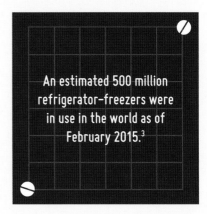

An estimated 500 million refrigerator-freezers were in use in the world as of February 2015.[3]

basic principle to design a refrigeration machine that used vapor instead of liquid. Evans, one of the most prolific inventors of his time, never built his refrigeration machine, perhaps because he was too busy inventing the first high-pressure steam engine and a predecessor to the automobile. This task fell to fellow American inventor Jacob Perkins, who began experimenting with refrigeration after moving to London, England, in the 1830s. In 1834, Perkins built a closed-loop system that moved heat from one place to another. Rather than release the gas into the air, the device pumped it away from the refrigeration area and compressed it again. The system released the heat into the outside air and pumped the gas back to begin the cycle again.

Jacob Perkins's closed-loop system advanced refrigeration.

JOHN GORRIE

John Gorrie was born in 1803 and spent most of his childhood in South Carolina. After receiving a degree in medicine, he moved to Apalachicola, Florida, a port city on the Gulf of Mexico. In addition to practicing medicine, Gorrie studied tropical diseases. Like most physicians of the time, Gorrie incorrectly believed malaria, yellow fever, and other diseases were caused by hot air—a theory that was supported by his observation that "nature would terminate the fevers by changing the seasons."[5] He wrote several articles urging people to drain swamps and marshlands, places where disease-carrying mosquitoes thrived. When Gorrie pursued the idea of using refrigeration to cool patients, he quickly discovered ice was expensive and sometimes hard to come by in the South, so he began exploring the potential of making artificial ice. By 1845, he quit practicing medicine to set about engineering an ice-making system. While receiving a US patent for his ice-making machine was a step forward, Gorrie's failure to succeed as a businessman because of circumstances, plus an early death, left him unknown in his day. He has since become renowned as a leading pioneer in refrigeration.

While Perkins received an English patent for his design, Gorrie received a US patent on May 6, 1851, for a machine that would "convert water into ice artificially by absorbing its heat of liquefaction with expanding air."[4] Gorrie's system moved water through a series of pipes, releasing heat and cooling the water to make ice.

A Chilly Reception

Gorrie's machine was not met with the same excitement as his chilled champagne. Few people felt the need for such a contraption. For many generations, people had relied on natural ice to keep things cool. Most people were used to

A diagram for Gorrie's ice machine, taken from his US patent

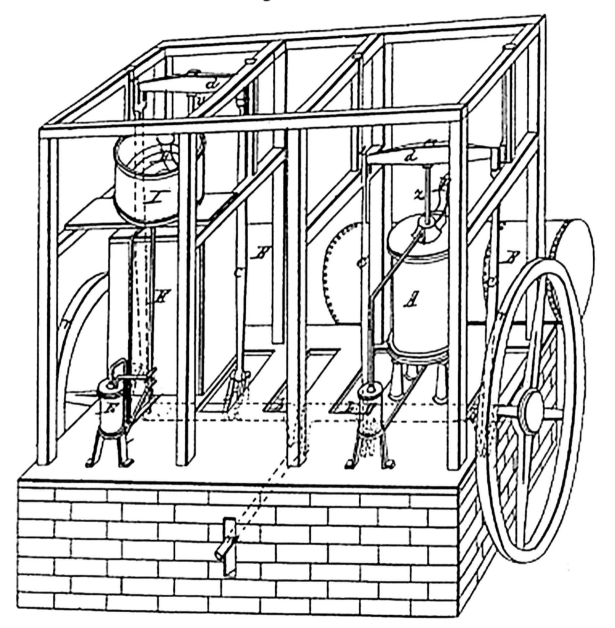

Fig: 1.

shopping daily for food. Those who could afford it had insulated iceboxes to keep food cool. In cities, workers delivered ice harvested from lakes and rivers daily, much as milk and butter were delivered at that time. The ice harvesting and delivery companies viewed Gorrie as a threat and set about discrediting his invention.

Critics pointed out that the machine was far too large for most businesses. They harped on performance issues that resulted from leaks in the cooling system. Rumors that ice was made instantly were quickly put to rest. The press mocked the ice-making machine as inconvenient, potentially dangerous, and even blasphemous. One *New York Globe* writer described Gorrie as a "crank . . . who thinks he can make ice by his machine as good as God almighty."[6]

The bad-mouthing and bad press did not help Gorrie. Then, only weeks after Gorrie received a patent for his ice machine, his business partner and chief investor died. In the midst of the negative press, other investors faded away. In 1855, at just 51 years old, Gorrie died penniless and brokenhearted. But his idea lived on.

Refrigeration Lives On

Gorrie's refrigeration machine may have been a market failure, but it inspired other inventors. Over the next several decades, creative minds in the United States, Europe, Australia, and elsewhere worked to invent a feasible refrigeration machine. Before long, refrigeration machines moved into the brewing and meatpacking industries and gradually into

A sculpture in Statuary Hall in Washington, DC, honors Gorrie as the father of refrigeration and air conditioning.

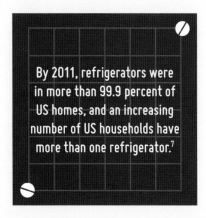

By 2011, refrigerators were in more than 99.9 percent of US homes, and an increasing number of US households have more than one refrigerator.[7]

the homes of consumers. As Gorrie did, subsequent inventors and companies would have to overcome skepticism about the refrigeration machines they promoted. But by the 1930s, the refrigerator would establish itself in US kitchens. From there, the refrigerator would grow in size and stature to become a must-have appliance throughout the world.

But refrigeration would become so much more. The technology would expand beyond the kitchen, allowing trains and trucks to move perishable goods with greater ease and less expense. Refrigeration would revolutionize agriculture and diet, affecting what, where, when, and how people eat. And refrigeration would evolve into air conditioning to cool more than food. Like the refrigerator appliance, air conditioning—built on the principles Gorrie introduced—would transform everyday life.

THE REFRIGERATOR

1000 BCE
The Chinese use ice from frozen waterways.

500 BCE
Egyptians and Indians set out containers of water at night to make ice through evaporation.

1748 CE
In Scotland, William Cullen demonstrates refrigeration through the evaporation of liquids in a vacuum.

ca. 1802
American businessman and inventor Thomas Moore receives a US patent for a "refrigerator," which is more accurately described as an icebox.

1834
American inventor Jacob Perkins introduces the first practical refrigerating machine, using ether in a vapor-compression cycle.

1851
American physician-turned-inventor John Gorrie receives a US patent for an ice-making machine.

1856
Scotsman James Harrison builds a machine to keep beer cold in an Australian brewery.

1873
In Munich, Germany, engineer Carl von Linde installs the first refrigeration system in a European brewery.

1877
Linde builds the first practical and portable compressor refrigeration machine.

1894
Linde develops a method for liquefying large quantities of gas that becomes known as the Linde technique and is central to refrigeration.

1904
Air conditioning makes its public debut at the Saint Louis World's Fair.

1910s
Air conditioning systems debut in movie theaters and department stores.

1913
American Fred W. Wolf introduces the first domestic refrigerator, the Domelre.

1915
American Alfred Mellowes designs the first self-contained refrigerator for home use.

1927
General Electric's "Monitor Top" becomes the first refrigerator to experience widespread household use.

CHAPTER 2

BEFORE THE
FRIDGE

For tens of thousands of years, people have recognized the value of refrigeration as a preservative. Bacteria, which exist in all food, cause food to spoil. Cooling food slows the growth of bacteria. For most of human history, the only method of cooling available to people was packing food in ice, snow, or frigid water. The method was far from foolproof. Well into the 1800s, people who succumbed to foodborne illnesses did not recognize food spoilage as their root cause. When and where it was hot, bacteria growth increased. Many who suffered from the resulting food poisoning mistakenly blamed the hot weather for bringing on what they called "summer complaint."[1]

A Roman relief depicts a butcher shop, which relied on a variety of ancient methods for preserving food, including smoking, drying, and salting.

Ice and Snow

Records show inhabitants of ancient China harvested ice by 1000 BCE. In China, and elsewhere, people brought down snow from the mountains or chipped ice from frozen waterways. In approximately 500 BCE, Egyptians began making ice by placing shallow earthenware pots containing water outside on cold nights. Similarly, in India, people made ice by keeping a thin layer of water in a shallow tray exposed to the night. Indians also kept the water cool by storing it in earthen pots that allowed for evaporation. As the water evaporated, it took the heat of the water remaining in the pot with it. In ancient Rome and Greece, people brought snow from the mountains and buried it in pits covered with straw or other insulating materials to slow melting.

For hundreds of years, these relatively primitive cooling methods remained the most advanced refrigeration technology available. The process began changing in the 1300s, when people in China discovered cold could be intensified by allowing salt water to evaporate. Fueled by increased trade between Asia and Europe, the method spread to Italy by 1500.

In Europe, people began experimenting with other ways to cool water. They found adding sodium nitrate, potassium nitrate, or other chemicals to water caused it to cool. In the 1600s, iced drinks became popular in the hot climates of southern Europe. This gave rise to a new cooling technique in which longneck bottles were rotated in water with potassium nitrate, or saltpeter, a substance that cooled the water as it dissolved.

In most places, however, collecting ice and snow remained the dominant source of refrigeration. And for a few enterprising individuals, it became a major source of income.

Sir Francis Bacon, an English statesman and philosopher, figured out that cold preserved meat. He began experimenting with the effect of refrigeration on poultry in 1626.

Ice Harvesting Becomes Big Business

In the United States, the ice harvesting business began in 1806, when New Englander Frederic Tudor attempted to ship ice to Martinique, an island in the Caribbean Sea. Tudor built an icehouse on the island and intended to sell the blocks of ice he had collected from the Hudson River to wealthy Europeans coping with the heat of the tropics. As ships traveled southward with Tudor's cargo, the heat took its toll. Slowly, the ice melted. When the ship arrived in port, less than one-half of the ice remained.

Tudor set about solving this problem. He embarked on a series of experiments to find better insulating materials. His efforts paid off. By the 1840s, from point of harvest to point of sale, Tudor's loss rate was less than 8 percent.[2] And Tudor was right about a ready market for ice. He steadily expanded his ice trade outward from Charleston, South

Men harvest ice in Pennsylvania in 1877.

Carolina, New Orleans, Louisiana, and Savannah, Georgia. Soon, he was making regular shipments throughout the southern United States, the Caribbean, and far beyond. He also sold to England, South America, China, Australia, and India, where the market was particularly strong.

Getting ice to customers was no easy feat. After cutting it from the Hudson, the ice traveled downriver by barge. Barges routinely carried between 400 and 800 short tons (360 and 730 metric tons) of ice.[3] The ice was stored belowdecks, where it was insulated by the cold river, much as the basement of a house is cooler because it is below ground. Barges also served as temporary storage facilities. Tudor also built aboveground insulated storage facilities to hold the ice before it was packed onto trains or ships.

Tudor became known as the "Ice King."[4] However, it was the ingenuity of fellow New Englander Nathaniel Wyeth that made possible many of the innovations in keeping things cold. During his lifetime, Wyeth received 14 patents related to ice cutting and storage. For example, he invented an icehouse with a double wall that had insulation between the walls. But it was his ice cutting methods that revolutionized the ice industry. In 1825, Wyeth introduced an efficient method by which horse-drawn carriages cut huge, uniform blocks of ice from ponds and rivers. The uniformity of the ice enabled ice companies to pack it more tightly. This not only allowed more ice to be packed into the limited space of a ship's cargo hold but also resulted in better insulation. The more densely packed a material is, the less it is exposed to air, which

ICE HARVESTING

Harvesting ice was difficult and often hazardous. Ice was thickest during the coldest hours of the night, so this is when harvesting often took place. The harvesters worked by the dim light of lanterns, which added to the danger. Men wore shoes with ice nails or "corks," tiny studs that helped give a little traction on the ice, but the men often fell anyway.[5] Horses were typically equipped with spiked horseshoes that made a kick potentially deadly. Early harvesting tools consisted of pickaxes, chisels, and handsaws—sharp tools made more dangerous because they easily slipped from cold, wet hands.

NATHANIEL WYETH

Nathaniel Wyeth had an inventive mind and entrepreneurial spirit. His creations included a horse-drawn ice cutter. Hoping to make it rich by shipping dried salmon to markets in the East, Wyeth led an expedition to Oregon in 1832, helping forge the path that would become the Oregon Trail. His travels were not easy. After losing most of his men to disease or violence, he returned to Boston, Massachusetts, in 1837 and resumed the ice business. He improved harvesting, transporting, and storing ice by making the tasks safer and more efficient.

can make it melt. Less melting translated into increased profits for ice companies.

The Ice Man Cometh

Some of the ice sold by ice harvesters cooled drinks, but most of it helped preserve food. In England and the United States, landowners built icehouses where huge sheets of ice were wrapped in wool, flannel, or straw. City dwellers did not have space for icehouses. Instead, refrigeration there took the form of an icebox, a small wooden box lined with metal—tin or zinc—and cooled with a block of ice, usually placed in a separate compartment at the top of the box. Users improved insulation by lining the inside of the icebox with sawdust, seaweed, or other materials. As cities grew, so did the distance between people and farms. While those who lived on farms often collected fresh produce every day, people in cities began shopping less often, relying increasingly on the icebox to keep meat, dairy, and produce fresh.

The iceboxes may have seemed like a modern convenience to city dwellers in the 1800s. But the invention was not foolproof. The iceboxes were relatively cold, but the temperature was still higher than today's experts recommend for refrigeration. Food spoilage was common, and iceboxes became rank and moldy. Even in the best-case scenario, food lasted just a couple days longer than it would without an icebox.

As the ice melted, its water dripped through an interior pipe into a collection pan underneath the icebox, on the floor. More expensive models used other methods for removing the water. Some had a spigot. Others had a pipe that delivered the water to a tank or to another pipe that sent the water elsewhere.

In addition to emptying the drip pans, users also had to replace the ice almost daily. This gave rise to a new business: ice delivery. By the mid-1800s, wagons delivering 25-, 50-, or 100-pound (11, 23, or 45 kg) blocks of ice door-to-door were a familiar sight in most US cities.

THE "MODERN" ICEBOX

Maryland businessman Thomas Moore designed the icebox to keep butter and milk cool during transport from Maryland's farms to customers in Washington, DC. In approximately 1802, he received a patent for his design, a wooden box with a tin chamber inside and insulated with rabbit fur along the exterior. Moore left room between the tin chamber and the wooden box for ice, which would keep the dairy products within the interior chamber cold. This icebox—which he called a refrigerator—remained virtually unchanged for almost a century, providing refrigeration long before the refrigerator known today took its place in the kitchen. The term *refrigerator* has come to mean an appliance that is cooled by mechanical refrigeration.

Customers placed cards in their windows telling the ice deliverer how many pounds of ice they wanted that day. The iceman used an ice pick to remove the desired amount and then carried the chunk on his back to put in the customer's icebox.

GLOBAL SUPPLY AND DEMAND

The United States was not the only country that harvested ice for export. In the late 1800s, Norway capitalized on its glaciers to supply ice to customers in Europe and beyond. More than half of the 1,000,000 short tons (900,000 metric tons) of ice exported annually from Norway went to Great Britain.[7]

Big Business Becomes Bigger

New ice harvesting companies sprang up to meet the growing demand for ice, and no pond, river, or stream was safe from the ravages of the ice industry. At the height of the market, Walden Pond in Massachusetts—which author Henry David Thoreau had esteemed for its natural beauty and tranquility—yielded an estimated 1,000 short tons (900 metric tons) of ice daily during the cold winter months.[6] New England's ice harvesters used techniques to increase the supply of natural ice. They drilled holes in the ice, which allowed water to reach the surface and freeze, thickening the ice. Elsewhere, workers cleared and dug out the land to create artificial ponds and lakes. The US ice business reached its peak in

A man delivers ice to a customer in an apartment building.

1872, when US exporters shipped more than 250,000 short tons (225,000 metric tons) of ice to countries as far away as China and Australia.[8]

As demand increased, relying on natural ice became a health problem. The rise of cities and industry contributed to sewage and pollution, and sources of clean ice became increasingly difficult to find. Warm winters made the problem worse—when rivers and ponds refused to freeze over, ice harvesters were at a loss for what to do. In the 1880s, higher-than-average temperatures created severe shortages of natural ice in the United States. The warm spell harmed the ice harvesting industry and fueled the drive to find alternatives.

Workers deliver ice using horse-drawn wagons circa 1900.

CHAPTER 3

FORERUNNERS TO THE
FRIDGE

Following Gorrie's failed attempt to sell his refrigeration machine, several entrepreneurs built on his ideas. Among the first was businessman Alexander C. Twining of Cleveland, Ohio. In 1856, he used his vapor-compression machine to produce ice artificially for commercial applications. That same year, James Harrison, a Scot living in Australia, received a patent for a vapor-compression system using ether, alcohol, or ammonia. That year, Harrison sold and installed the first vapor-compression refrigeration machine in an Australian brewery. Harrison's machine

Refrigeration technology changed the brewing industry.

was huge, powered by a flywheel that was 16 feet (4.9 m) in diameter. The machine produced approximately 6,600 pounds (3,000 kg) of ice a day.[1]

Other breweries also capitalized on mechanical refrigeration. In some places, high-quality ice was hard to get. Ice from different frozen ponds or lakes varied in quality. Making their own ice enabled breweries to create a more standard product year-round. Moreover, the breweries could keep their beer cold. The taste of beer changes when it is warm, so refrigeration meant consistently fresher-tasting beers. Refrigeration technology offered breweries a significant return on investment by improving efficiency. For the first time, brewers could make cold beer year-round and keep it cold.

Then, in 1859, French engineer Ferdinand Carré introduced a continuous absorption refrigeration system. Although absorption refrigeration is based on similar principles as compression refrigeration, it uses another liquid, such as a solution of lithium bromide and water, to absorb the refrigerant after it has been transformed from liquid to gas. In comparison, the compression system uses a mechanical compressor to increase pressure on the gas and then condenses the hot high-pressure gas back to a liquid by heat exchange with air or another coolant.

Ice Plants

When the American Civil War (1861–1865) cut off the supply of natural ice from the North to the South, Carré found a market for his ice machine. The first Carré machine slipped past a Union blockade to land in Mexico and eventually made its way to San Antonio, Texas. In 1868, a group of New Orleans entrepreneurs formed the Louisiana Ice Manufacturing Company. The company used Carré's machines to freeze water to distribute ice to local customers. Other ice plants soon sprang up across the South, breaking the monopoly of the northeastern ice harvesters.

By the early 1900s, ice was so vital that working in an ice plant excused a man from the draft during World War I (1914–1918) and World War II (1941–1945).

Most of the early ice plants were built in southern states, where there was no ice to be harvested. Following the Civil War, the South wanted to remain as independent as possible from the North. Despite initial skepticism about the "artificial" ice

ARTIFICIAL ICE RINKS

Advances in refrigeration led to artificial ice rinks. In 1870, William Newton constructed in New York City what is widely considered the first ice rink. To produce the ice and keep it frozen, Newton used a huge vapor-compression system directly under the water. In 1876, a mechanically refrigerated ice surface was installed in London. This consisted of a small, 100-square-foot (9 sq m) surface cooled by copper pipes in which ether chilled a mixture of glycerin and water. These earliest ice rinks were small, and the ice melted quickly, but they set the stage for later designs. By the first decade of the 1900s, several US cities had built ice rinks. This contributed to the rapid growth of the National Hockey League, which formed in 1917.

Circa 1920, the Christian Heurich Brewing Company's ice plant in Washington, DC, was busy.

produced by these plants, by the early 1900s, such ice had largely replaced harvested ice in many, if not most, parts of the country.

By 1900, the United States had 766 ice plants. Still, the ice machine astounded many people. In the 2010 *Mississippi History Now* article "Making Ice in Mississippi," Elli Morris wrote about the experience of a country preacher who visited an ice plant in Jackson, Mississippi, in 1902. When he returned home and described the ice plant to his congregation, "the good people of his faith decided either the preacher had lost his mind or had been taken in by the devil himself. They kindly asked him to step down from his post for making such an outlandish statement that ice could be made in Mississippi in July."[2]

Ice Making Becomes an Industry

Not all ice is the same. Because air bubbles and impurities increase the melting rate of ice, icemen sought to produce clear ice. This required the water to be in constant motion as it froze. It took an average of three days to make a 300-pound (136 kg) block of ice, which was the standard size of ice produced by most ice plants.

Artificial ice makers used advertising and marketing techniques to boost sales and to capitalize on concerns about pollution and natural ice. Producers of new mechanical ice-making equipment used distilled water—the water has been converted to a vapor and then back into liquid form—which resulted in cleaner ice. A 1904 British report commissioned by the London County Council confirmed that artificial ice was more hygienic than even the purest natural ice, due to the threat of contamination during transport and storage of harvested ice, which usually traveled long distances, while artificial ice tended to be used locally.

Still, blocks of artificial ice made their way into homes the same way as harvested ice. From the ice plants, ice wagons carried the ice to city streets and customers. These wagons were pulled by mules that, according to Morris,

FISHING AND ICE

The huge blocks of ice made by ice companies in the early 1900s helped fuel the US seafood industry along the East Coast and the Gulf of Mexico. Fishermen put chipped block ice into the hulls of their trawlers and lay their catch atop the ice. Preserving the fish this way enabled the fishing boats to stay at sea longer and fish farther from shore.

MISPLACED DELIVERY

Ice and iceboxes became common among upper-class Americans but remained novelties for many. The wife of an ice plant manager in Friars Point, Mississippi, once recalled a story about an ice deliveryman who had his son fill in for him one day. The ice deliverer did not have an icebox, so his son was unfamiliar with what they looked like. Eager to please, the son made the rounds to deliver the huge blocks of ice where they needed to go. After he returned to the warehouse, however, the owner received a call from a customer who complained she had not received her ice. The son insisted he had made the delivery—a fact confirmed by the plant manager. There was just one problem. He had left it in the oven, not the icebox.

"learned the delivery routes so well they didn't need a driver. Instead, the iceman stayed in the back of the wagon, hopping out when the mule stopped at the right location."[3]

Refrigeration Goes Commercial

Refrigeration techniques affected other areas of society. In addition to cooling food, technology advanced to cool entire buildings. The first cold-storage warehouses were built in the 1860s in Boston, New York, Cleveland, and Indianapolis, Indiana, primarily to preserve fruit. Huge blocks of ice packed in straw or sawdust kept these warehouses cool.

Refrigeration machines soon became standard in the brewery and meatpacking industries. In 1870, S. Liebmann's Sons Brewing Company in Brooklyn, New York, became one of the first US businesses to install a refrigeration machine. In 1873, German professor of mechanical engineering Carl von Linde, who contributed to many advances in the science of refrigeration, made the Spaten Brewery of Munich, Germany,

CARL VON LINDE

Carl von Linde was one of the visionaries behind refrigeration. After building a vapor-compression system for the Spaten Brewery in Munich in 1873, Linde looked for a way to make a practical portable refrigerating machine. His research led to the invention of the first reliable portable compressed-ammonia refrigerator, which he introduced to the market in 1877. To manufacture and market his invention, he established the *Gesellschaft für Lindes Eismaschinen Aktiengesellschaft*, or Society for Lindes Ice Machines. Linde was every bit as much a businessman as an engineer. By 1890, he had sold 747 machines to breweries and slaughterhouses.[4] His company, Linde AG, remains a leading manufacturer of refrigerators in Europe, while companies formed to use Linde's patents have become some of the largest chemical companies in the world. His breakthrough discovery in gas liquefaction in 1894, known as the Linde technique, continues to serve as the basis for refrigeration today and earned Linde the 1913 Nobel Prize in physics.

the first European brewery to have a refrigeration system. By 1890, a brewery operating without some kind of refrigeration was rare.

Refrigeration came next to the meatpacking industry. In the 1800s, meat processing was inefficient. Between the slaughterhouse and the customer, meat would go through several middlemen: the packer, the distributor, and the butcher. Each step in the process meant the meat was getting older and less fresh. Because meat could be kept only a short time before it would spoil, it was typically preserved by soaking it in brine. Because cold extended the life of the meat, the vast majority of meat processing was done during winter. Fresh meat was rare except during winter and was virtually unheard of at any time of the year in some places.

As had breweries before them, meatpackers began enlisting the help of engineers to build insulated cold rooms and cooling systems. In 1871, the first mechanically refrigerated slaughterhouse in the United States was built in Fulton, Texas. One by one, the meatpackers purchased and installed elaborate, expensive refrigeration machines to cool their processing plants and enable them to extend their business year-round. As westward expansion contributed to a growing livestock industry in the West, businesses built refrigerated packing plants to preserve the meat as it made its way to population centers in the East. But getting the meat from one stop to another still took time. Advances in railroads helped people and goods travel to a growing number of places, but before trains could be used for meat, someone had to develop a system to keep the meat cold.

By 1920, manufactured ice was a $1 billion industry and ranked ninth in the amount of investment among US commercial enterprises.[5]

COLD-STORAGE WAREHOUSES

Some of the cold-storage warehouses were independent entities, but the meatpackers, dairies, and fruit wholesalers also built their own cold-storage warehouses. These multistory buildings transformed the urban skyline. They were also uniquely American. Cities elsewhere in the world had fewer refrigerator railcars to transport goods and fewer cold-storage warehouses to keep goods fresh. As a result, only in the United States could the average consumer access fresh, seasonal foods year-round.

Carl von Linde's refrigeration machine

HOW REFRIGERATION
WORKS

Refrigeration is the process of removing heat from an enclosed space to lower its temperature. Refrigeration can take place in a space of any size, from the small refrigerators common in college dorm rooms to massive versions in giant warehouses. When refrigeration is used to keep rooms or buildings comfortably cool for people, it is called air conditioning.

A vapor-compression machine refrigerates through the evaporation of a substance called a refrigerant. Refrigerants evaporate at exceptionally low temperatures. 1. Compression of low-pressure refrigerant vapor in the compressor increases the pressure and temperature of the refrigerant vapor. 2. The hot high-pressure vapor is cooled in the condenser to form a medium-temperature liquid. 3. This liquid expands through an expansion valve to a low pressure and temperature mixture of refrigerant liquid and vapor. 4. This cold liquid-vapor refrigerant mixture then enters the evaporator, in which the liquid boils while absorbing heat from the warm air flowing over the evaporator, cooling the air. 5. A fan keeps the air moving over the evaporator to produce continuous cooling, or refrigeration.

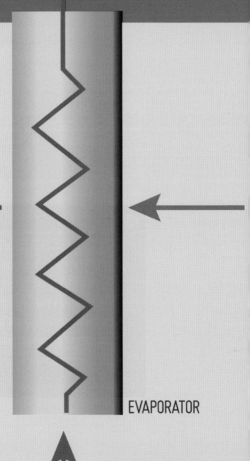

COLD AIR

EVAPORATOR

4. LIQUID + VAPOR
(LOW TEMPERATURE)

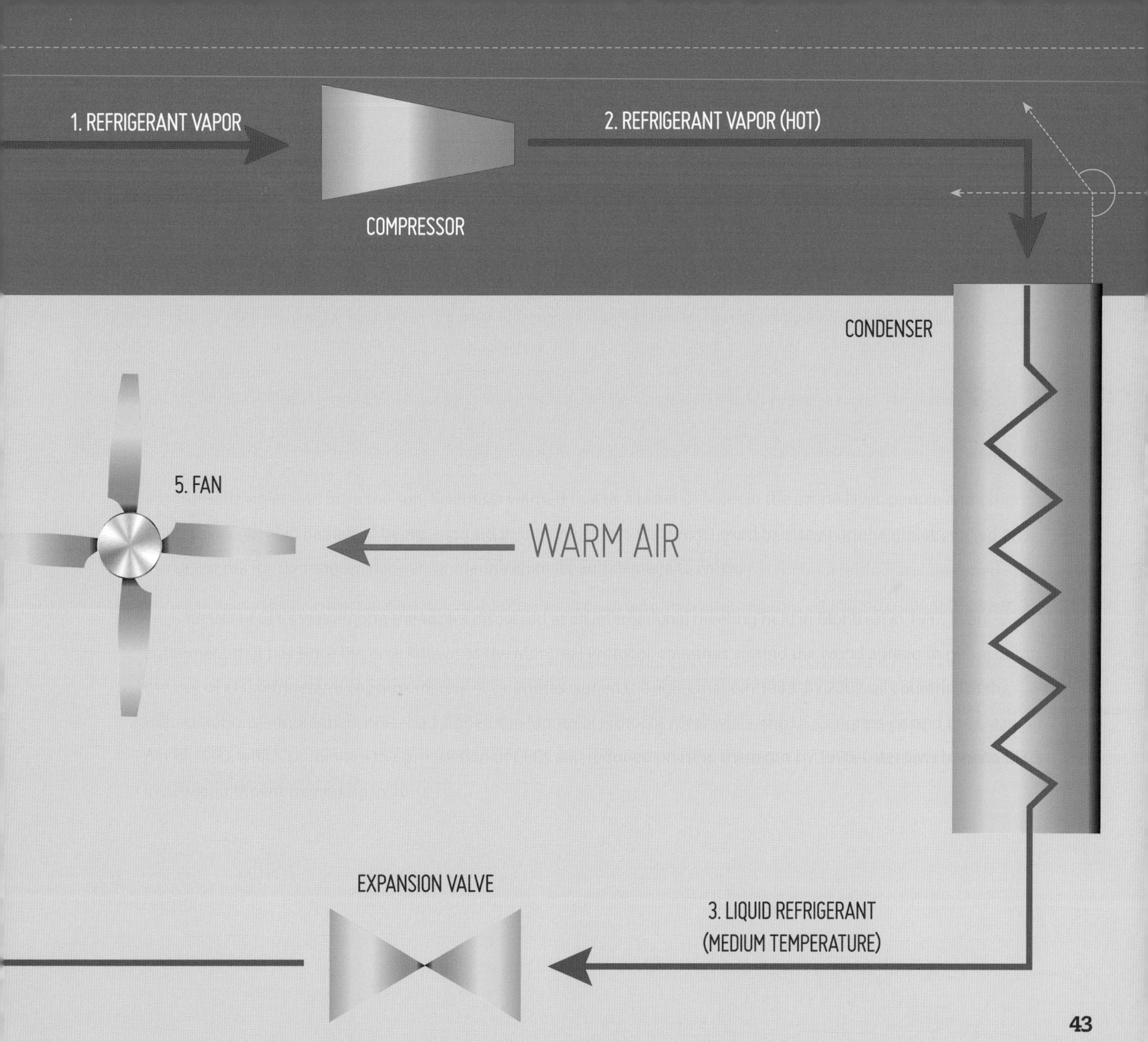

1. REFRIGERANT VAPOR

COMPRESSOR

2. REFRIGERANT VAPOR (HOT)

CONDENSER

5. FAN

WARM AIR

EXPANSION VALVE

3. LIQUID REFRIGERANT
(MEDIUM TEMPERATURE)

43

CHAPTER 4

REFRIGERATED TRANSPORT

Refrigeration in transportation paralleled the advances in refrigeration systems in processing plants and warehouses. The earliest refrigerated railcars packed milk and butter in ice harvested from ponds and rivers. By the mid-1800s, insulated railcars transported a wide variety of goods, including seafood from New England to the mid-Atlantic and meat from Chicago to Boston. In the 1860s, horticulturist Parker Earle started Illinois Central Railroad's "strawberry express," which transported strawberries from the farms of southern Illinois to Chicago and beyond in huge insulated boxes cooled by 100 pounds (45 kg) of ice.[1] Other fruit growers soon followed Earle's example, and fresh produce began

Workers ice spinach before loading it into a refrigerator car in Texas in 1939.

EARLY PROBLEMS WITH SHIPPING MEAT

Meatpackers experimented with a number of strategies for refrigerating meat in transit before hitting on one that would work. In 1857, meatpackers attempted to ship beef in ordinary boxcars that had bins of ice. The beef was placed directly on the ice. Because the meat placed directly on the ice was much colder than the layers above, the temperature of the meat was inconsistent. The meat in direct contact with the ice froze, even as some of the other meat spoiled. In addition, freezing meat dehydrates it, which causes red meat to turn grayish brown, making it less appealing.

popping up at groceries and farmers' markets in areas throughout the country.

The Rise of the Reefer

The early railcars were problematic. The huge chunks of ice had to be replaced daily and made a swampy mess as they melted. Too often, the produce spoiled along the way, cutting into profits. Entrepreneurs sought better alternatives. In 1867, J. B. Sutherland of Detroit, Michigan, patented the first refrigerator railcar, which soon became known as a "reefer."[2] He described the car in his patent application as a "double-walled, double-roofed, and double-floored car as to ensure constant circulation of air within the car, so that warmed air is conducted through ice-chests, and, thus cooled, returned to the body of the car."[3] Ice bunkers on either end of the car held approximately 800 pounds (360 kg) of ice.[4] Flaps allowed for the circulation of air, which improved cooling over previous refrigerated cars. In addition, hatches in the roof provided access to the bunkers on either end, which made it easier to replace the ice.

Despite its advantages for transporting perishable goods, railroad companies hesitated in adopting refrigeration technologies. Refrigerated railcars were heavy and more expensive than standard boxcars. Their interiors were smaller because, of necessity, some of the space was taken up by ice. This meant they could carry less product. Railroad companies viewed buying cars that could carry just one type of commodity as a poor investment. While boxcars carried other commodities on return trips, most refrigerator cars returned empty. Companies had already invested heavily in stock cars and stockyards to move livestock along their lines and were not eager to encourage shipping beef instead.

As a result, meatpackers stepped in to establish their own refrigerated rail lines. In 1878, Chicago cattle dealer Gustavus Swift invested in a fleet of ice-cooled railcars designed by engineer Andrew Chase and built by the Michigan Car Company. Swift followed by establishing his own line of refrigerated cars, the Swift Refrigerator Line, which allowed him to expand his business across the nation. He began with a fleet of ten cars. By 1903, his fleet had expanded to 5,900 cars.[5] Soon, Chicago's other meatpackers followed suit, and special cars sporting the colors and logos of the

The Morris Company relied on a refrigerated truck in 1918 to keep its meats cold during delivery.

meatpackers became a common sight along the nation's railways. The five major Chicago meatpackers controlled an estimated 90 percent of the refrigerated rail transport in the United States.[6]

Fresh Meat and Produce

Refrigerated railcars enabled produce to travel hundreds of miles. By the end of the 1800s, reefers were carrying a wide range of perishables from farm to city and from coast to coast. Improvements in the design of the reefers continued. While earlier cars had to be repeatedly filled with ice along a route, later cars used fans powered by electricity to force cool air around the load. Combined with the expansion of the railroad industry, the new refrigeration technologies allowed breweries, meatpackers, dairy producers, and fruit and vegetable growers to reach faraway consumers.

ANDREW CHASE IMPROVES MEAT SHIPPING

Gustavus Swift experimented with shipping meat from Chicago to New York during the winter months in boxcars with their doors removed, but the solution only worked during the coldest winter weather, making it impractical. In 1868, William Davis of Detroit received a patent for a design that used metal racks. Carcasses could hang from the racks above ice that contained salt, which melted the ice faster. This decreased the average temperature. While this kept the meat cool, the shifting weight of swinging carcasses caused numerous derailments. Swift hired Andrew Chase to find a solution. Chase solved this problem by positioning the meat at the bottom of the railcar and the ice at the top. As the air circulated over the ice, it cooled. Because cooler air is heavier than warmer air, it dropped into the refrigerator car and forced warmer air out of the car through ventilators in the floor. Moreover, because the meat was no longer hanging, the center of gravity was lowered. With no dramatic shifts in weight, the cars were steady on the rails. Chase's design fed the improvement and success of refrigerated railcars.

Local farmers no longer had to grow all the crops area residents wanted, and regions began to specialize in the crops best suited to their unique climate and soil, such as peaches in Georgia. Large farming areas sprang up in remote regions. The citrus and vegetable industries of the Southwest were among the early beneficiaries of refrigerated transport.

Refrigerated rail also transformed the US diet. Access to fresh produce meant diets became more varied and more nutritious. Fresh produce shipped northward helped to virtually eliminate scurvy, a once-common disease caused by

AGRICULTURAL SPECIALIZATION

The advent of refrigerated transportation contributed to regions specializing in certain products. Meatpacking became centralized in Chicago, while the Midwest quickly became known for its dairy. Georgia became known for its peaches, Mississippi for its tomatoes, and the Gulf states for strawberries. Florida was able to ship its citrus north, making the fruit a central part of the Florida economy. But it may have been California that benefited most from refrigerated rail early on. California's climate proved suitable for a wide range of produce. Reefers soon carried the bounty from California's fruit orchards, vineyards, and vegetable gardens across sparsely populated territory to ready markets in the East.

vitamin C deficiency. In addition, people could live farther away from farms and still get fresh food, which fueled the growth of cities.

Intercontinental Shipping

On the other side of the world, people were trying to figure out a way to export beef to markets in Great Britain. James Harrison, who had built refrigeration machines for a number of Australian breweries and meatpacking plants, had shown meat kept frozen for months was safe to eat. He believed shipping meat to England could prove to be a highly profitable enterprise. To this end, Harrison equipped a ship called the *Norfolk* with a room meant to be kept cold with ice. In 1873, the *Norfolk* set sail from Australia to Great Britain carrying frozen beef packed in ice. By the time it arrived in Great Britain, however, the ice had melted and the beef was spoiled.

William Soltau Davidson, who had emigrated from Great Britain to New Zealand, succeeded where Harrison had failed. In 1881, he arranged for the installation of a vapor-compression refrigeration system on the *Dunedin*. The next year, the ship sailed for London with frozen meat in the cargo hold. Unlike more modest advances in refrigerated transport, Davidson's success caught the attention of the media. A *London Times* reporter wrote about the *Dunedin*'s successful voyage:

> *Today we have to record such a triumph over physical difficulties as would have been incredible, and even unimaginable, a very few days ago.... We seem only just now to have arrived at the certainty that meat can be brought in good condition a mere week's voyage across the Atlantic in the most temperate of the earth's zones. The present arrival is by a sailing ship after a passage of ninety-eight days across the tropics; indeed for a large part of the voyage in heat which Englishmen find almost intolerable.[7]*

Within a year, several other ships carried beef from New Zealand to markets in Great Britain and beyond. Refrigerated shipping increased the supply of meat and dairy throughout the world, bringing down prices and contributing to a worldwide boom in the sale and consumption of meat and dairy products.

"Refrigeration brought distant production centers and the North American population together. It tore down the barriers of climates and seasons. And while it helped to rev up industrial processes, it became an industry itself."[8]

—*Barbara Krasner-Khait*, History Magazine, *Feb./Mar. 2000*

In an article published in August 1929, the *Ladies' Home Journal*, a magazine for women, enthusiastically endorsed the changes brought about by refrigeration:

Refrigeration wipes out seasons and distances. Duluth serves California or Florida orange juice for breakfast, Buffalo school children munch bananas from South America, Chicago dines on roast Long Island duckling. We grow perishable products in the regions best suited to them instead of being forced to stick close to the large markets.[9]

In the United States, refrigerated railcars remained the predominant method of carrying perishable goods until the 1950s, when the interstate highway system fueled the growth of trucking.

Because of refrigerated ships and reefers, the middle classes had access to foods from thousands of miles away, and the rich could buy exotic foods that traveled from the far reaches of the earth. But a new problem emerged. Getting the food was not enough. People needed a way to preserve it. The market was right for a home refrigerator appliance.

The *Dunedin* in port in 1882

CHAPTER 5

AIR CONDITIONING IS BORN

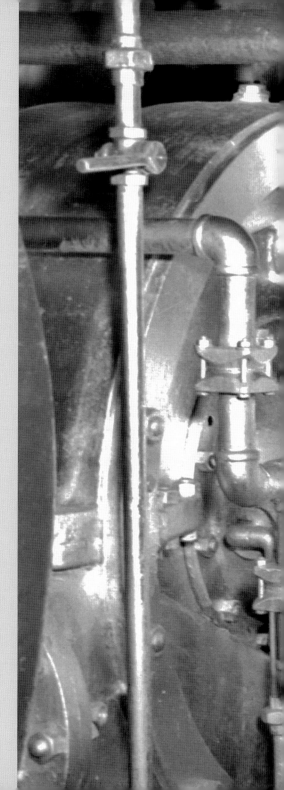

While much of refrigeration's history has focused on the refrigerator, inventors and scientists have looked for applications beyond food preservation. In the 1840s, Gorrie's goal for refrigeration was to cool the air for people, not food or drink. Others would take up Gorrie's cause. Around 1900, a young American engineer named Willis Haviland Carrier would earn the moniker "father of air conditioning" for his success in making air conditioning practical for businesses and homes.[1]

Carrier's experiments came at the request of his employer, the Buffalo Forge Company. The Sackett & Wilhelms Lithography and

Willis Carrier in 1922 with the first "chiller" air conditioner he invented

Printing Company, a printing plant in Brooklyn, New York, had asked Buffalo Forge to find a solution to its humidity problem. Humidity causes paper to expand and contract. As a result, ink, when applied one color at a time, may not align. This hampered efficiency at the plant and caused waste.

Carrier, a recent engineering graduate of Cornell University, was 25 years old when he introduced his invention. His inspiration came on a foggy, misty train platform. "If I can saturate air and control its temperature at saturation, I can get air with any amount of moisture I want in it," Carrier thought. "I can do it, too, by drawing the air through a fine spray of water to create actual fog."[2]

Carrier created an apparatus that replaced steam in heating coils with cold water. Lowering the temperature to the desired dew point (the temperature at which moisture in the air forms drops) required balancing the temperature of the coil surface with the rate of airflow. In 1902, Sackett & Wilhelms, the printing company, installed the first system using Carrier's design. The system maintained a constant humidity of 55 percent and had the equivalent cooling effect of melting 108,000 pounds (48,988 kg) of ice per day.[3] A writer for the Carrier website explained the importance of the system:

Carrier's air-conditioning system helped solve the problem of humidity that plagued printers.

This new design was so different—so novel . . . it would not only help to solve a problem that had long plagued printers, but would one day launch a company and create an entire industry essential to global productivity and personal comfort.[4]

Cooling Rooms and Buildings

Refrigeration also merged with another American phenomenon—the movies. In the midst of the summer heat in the southeastern United States, early movie theaters kept their patrons cool by placing a large block of ice in front of a fan. Particularly in the South, the movie industry quickly recognized the power of comfort in luring people into theaters. By the 1910s, movie theater owners attracted moviegoers with marquees that announced, "It's 20 degrees cooler inside."[5] Mechanical refrigeration followed, and patrons began expecting the movie theater would be comfortably cool.

Keeping entire rooms cool with ice was not easy. A number of engineers and entrepreneurs saw the potential of adapting the mechanical refrigeration techniques used to keep food cool to cool the air. American engineer Alfred Wolff was among the pioneers of the technology. In 1902, Wolff installed a cooling machine that weighed 300 short tons (270 metric tons) in the New York Stock Exchange, making it the first multistory building in the world to be cooled by air conditioning. Air conditioning received a public debut at the 1904 World's Fair in Saint Louis, Missouri, where a massive mechanical refrigeration system cooled the Missouri State Building.

CARRIER CORPORATION

In 1915, Willis Carrier established the Carrier Engineering Corporation, which became the Carrier Corporation in 1930. Since its founding, the company has been a leading provider of air conditioning systems for homes and businesses. It has also been an innovator in the field of air conditioning. In the 1950s, air conditioning made a new shopping experience—the shopping mall—possible, with stores facing inward, toward an enclosed and air-conditioned court.

In 1993, Carrier Corporation helped preserve some of the world's most valuable artwork, which can be damaged by too much humidity. That year, Carrier installed units to precisely measure humidity in the Sistine Chapel, in Rome, Italy, where, in the early 1500s, famous Renaissance artist Michelangelo painted the walls and ceilings with frescoes of biblical stories. The technology was designed to cool a maximum of 700 visitors. In 2014, Carrier installed a new system designed to meet the demand of the popular tourist attraction, which gets as many as 20,000 visitors a day.[6] The new system is intended to cool 2,000 people at a time.

Textiles and Beyond

Stuart H. Cramer, a southern textile mill engineer, recognized the advantages of Carrier's system. Cramer believed adding humidity would help to condition yarn so it would not break. He received a patent for a device that would add water vapor to the air. Being able to control humidity allowed cotton spinning plants to increase their efficiency. Because yarn moves at such high speeds in a textile plant, even small changes in flexibility or strength affect output and production. At a 1906 meeting of the American Cotton Manufacturers, Cramer introduced the term *air conditioning*, which he defined to include humidifying as well as evaporative cooling. That same year, American

KEEPING COOL WHILE TRAVELING

In 1930, the Baltimore & Ohio Railroad tested the ability of a Carrier centrifugal chiller to cool one of its dining cars by heating the car to 93 degrees Fahrenheit (34°C) and then turning on the air conditioner. Within 20 minutes, the temperature of the dining car dropped to a comfortable 73 degrees Fahrenheit (23°C), marking the advent of air conditioning in passenger rail.[7] In 1932, the Chesapeake & Ohio Railroad installed air conditioning on the *George Washington*, which ran between New York and Washington, DC. In 1936, United Air Lines introduced air conditioning in its passenger planes. In 1939, Packard became the first automobile company to offer air conditioning, adding the optional feature at the cost of $274. By 1969, air conditioning was a standard feature in 54 percent of all new cars.[8]

architect Frank Lloyd Wright incorporated air conditioning into his design for the Larkin Administration Building in Buffalo, New York, making it the first office building specifically designed to accommodate air conditioning.

Both Cramer and Carrier sold their units to businesses throughout the United States. Carrier also continued improving on his system. In 1921, he patented a refrigeration machine that used a centrifugal compressor to force refrigerant through the system. Prior to this, air conditioning had depended on huge piston-driven compressors. Carrier's design for what became known as the centrifugal chiller was the first practical method for controlling the temperature and humidity of large spaces. It extended the reach of modern air conditioning beyond industry. In 1924, the J. L. Hudson Department Store in Detroit installed three Carrier centrifugal air conditioning units. Recognizing the appeal to shoppers, other department stores soon followed suit. The centrifugal chiller also brought air conditioning to other environments, including passenger trains, and, later, airplanes.

Cool Comfort at Home

In 1926, Carrier developed a residential air conditioner. It was intended for private homes. Not long after, several companies were offering in-home systems. Air conditioning was expanded further by the window unit. In 1947, more than 43,000 window air conditioners were sold in the United States.[9] Home air conditioning continued to spread with the postwar housing boom. By the late 1960s, most new houses were built with central air conditioning.

Air conditioning had a profound impact on settlement patterns. The US population shifted

A Carrier air conditioner cools a house in New Jersey.

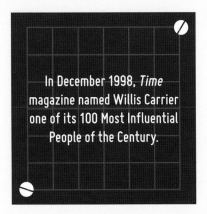

In December 1998, *Time* magazine named Willis Carrier one of its 100 Most Influential People of the Century.

dramatically, moving toward the South and Southwest. Florida, Georgia, Texas, New Mexico, Arizona, and Southern California experienced above-average growth once air conditioning took hold in the late 1900s. In 1950, 28 percent of the population lived in the Sunbelt. In 2000, the number was 40 percent.[10] Experts credit the change in large part to air conditioning. Beyond the United States, it is unlikely that places such as Dubai—the largest city of the United Arab Emirates, which was built within a desert—would have emerged without artificial cooling.

A General Electric air conditioner advertisement circa 1941

GENERAL *GE* ELECTRIC

FIND OUT
HOW LITTLE
IT COSTS TO
Sleep
IN COMFORT
Work
IN COMFORT
Play
IN COMFORT
THE WHOLE
YEAR 'ROUND

IT FILTERS
*
IT CIRCULATES
*
IT BRINGS IN
FRESH AIR
*
IT MUFFLES
NOISES
*
IT COOLS
*
IT
DEHUMIDIFIES

573560   G-E WINDOW DISPLAY "546-3" FOR ROOM AIR CONDITIONERS.

FILING NO. 9934   E318.67   E300.9   5-6-41

CHAPTER 6

THE FRIDGE
COMES HOME

1924

M-9

FRIGIDAIRE

THE FIRST
METAL CABINET
•
AIR-COOLED
COMPRESSOR
•
THE FIRST
COIL FREEZER
HAS REPLACED
THE BRINE TANK

In the late 1800s, ice continued growing in popularity. People found it was good for cooling food and chilling drinks. At the turn of the 1900s, a number of companies from many different industries raced to build a practical mechanical refrigerator that could replace the icebox in homes. As manufacturers built on one another's innovations, the refrigerator became increasingly practical. Before that happened, though, inventors had to resolve several issues.

Size was a major challenge. The refrigeration systems used in breweries, slaughterhouses, and ice plants were behemoths that sometimes weighed more than 100 short tons (90 metric tons).[1]

1928
AP-9
FRIGIDAIRE

THE FIRST ALL
PORCELAIN CABINET,
THE LIFETIME FINISH.
THE FIRST COLD CONTROL
TO LOWER OR RAISE
TEMPERATURES.
THE FIRST HYDRATOR
FOR KEEPING
VEGETABLES CRISP
AND FRESH.

1933
STANDARD 6-33
FRIGIDAIRE

A RADICALLY NEW
COMPRESSOR THAT USED
NO MORE CURRENT THAN
AN ORDINARY LIGHT
BULB...THE FORERUNNER
OF THE NOW WORLD
FAMOUS METER-MISER
F-114 REFRIGERANT.
THE FIRST AUTOMATIC
RESET DEFROSTER.
THE FIRST AUTOMATIC
TRAY RELEASE

A collection of early Frigidaire electric refrigerators

MARY ENGLE PENNINGTON

Mary Engle Pennington was a bacteriological chemist who focused much of her attention on the use of refrigeration for food safety. In the 1890s—when it was highly unusual for women to attend college—Pennington received a PhD from the University of Pennsylvania. She went on to conduct postdoctoral research in chemical botany at the university and then in physiological chemistry at Yale.

In 1904, Pennington accepted a job with the city of Philadelphia, Pennsylvania, where she was responsible for ensuring the safety of dairy products. Pennington set about educating dairy farmers, ice cream vendors, and others about the dangers of bacteria. Pennington went on to work for the US Department of Agriculture, where she pioneered research in refrigeration and how it could be used to keep food safe from bacteria. She also designed refrigerated boxcars with sufficient insulation to keep food cold during their journey. Pennington later worked for a company that made refrigerator insulation before becoming a consultant and continuing to explore and educate others about the use of refrigeration for food safety.

And the steam engines that powered them took up additional space. As inventors cast about for solutions for home use, they tried installing the steam-driven compressor in the basement and piping cold air to an insulated iceless box in the kitchen. In addition to their size, these early designs were noisy. They created a loud and constant hum that was audible several rooms and several floors away.

Engineers also had to overcome obstacles to safe and efficient operation. The commercial systems required ongoing maintenance and supervision. The machines leaked and often allowed toxic fumes from refrigerants—ammonia, sulfur dioxide, or methyl chloride—to escape. News reports of fires and explosions scared away even the bravest consumers. In 1893, for instance, a fire broke out in the cold storage building at the World's Columbian Exposition in Chicago, a highly publicized event organized to celebrate the four-hundredth anniversary of Christopher Columbus's landing in the Americas. Built by Hercules Iron Works and the Ice and Refrigeration Machine Manufacturers, the warehouse provided cold storage for the fair's many food vendors and doubled as an ice-skating rink. As thousands of onlookers watched, 17 people—12 of them Chicago firefighters—perished in the flames.[2] Considering the building was touted as an engineering marvel, the event heightened concerns about the safety of refrigeration technology.

Frigidaire

With ingenuity, experimentation, and hard work, dedicated inventors overcame the engineering hurdles and won over the public. In 1901, Henry Trost, an engineer in Albany, New York, received a US patent for a refrigerator designed for domestic use. Trost's refrigerator improved on previous icebox designs by putting the food compartment between cold-air boxes.

General Electric (GE) combined cold storage with mechanical ice making. In 1911, GE unveiled a refrigerator based on the work of Marcel Audiffen, a French monk who designed his airtight refrigeration system to cool wine. GE made two of these refrigerators at a cost of $1,000 each.[3] The price tag for the GE refrigerator made the appliance unobtainable for many consumers.

THE HUMIDITY PROBLEM

Humidity was a problem with early refrigerators. Cold circulating air sucked moisture as well as heat from meat and vegetables. When the refrigerator door was closed, moist air caused condensation that dripped onto food and ultimately ruined it. After much trial and error, refrigerator engineers finally found a solution by adding a motor that ran a fan to control air circulation inside the refrigerator. Providing air circulation inside the refrigerator reduces the internal humidity.

Eventually, makers added the crisper, a refrigerator drawer or compartment designed to keep fresh fruits and vegetables crisp, or fresh, by controlling the level of humidity. Because different foods need different levels of humidity, many of today's refrigerator models come with crispers that have separate temperature and humidity controls. In general, vegetables need more moisture than fruits. Today's crisper drawers have a fruit or vegetable setting that traps the optimal level of moisture.

Two years later, in 1913, American engineer Fred W. Wolf introduced the Domestic Electric Refrigerator—or Domelre. The Domelre ran on electricity and put an air-conditioned refrigeration unit atop an icebox. The Domelre was also the first refrigerating system to feature a tray for making ice cubes.

In 1915, Alfred Mellowes, an American engineer, designed the first self-contained refrigeration unit in which the compressor—or refrigeration machine—resided inside the appliance, at the bottom of the cabinet. To manufacture his refrigerator, Mellowes and a group of investors founded Guardian Refrigerator, which began operations in Detroit in 1916. The company struggled with production. By 1917, after two years, Guardian had managed to build only

40 machines.[4] In 1918, W. C. Durant, the president of the automobile company General Motors (GM), privately purchased Mellowes's company.

Durant changed the name of Guardian Refrigerator to Frigidaire and brought several automobile innovations—chief among them, the assembly line—to the manufacture of refrigerators. The first Frigidaire rolled off the assembly line in September 1918 in Detroit. GM expanded its competitive edge by purchasing the patent to the Domelre a few years later, which limited competitors' ability to copy the design.

Increased Competition

Other manufacturers—including GE and Kelvinator, founded in 1914 in Detroit by engineer Nathaniel B.

Fred W. Wolf's Domestic Electric Refrigerator, or Domelre

DEVELOPMENT OF THE ICE CREAM CABINET

The first electrically refrigerated ice cream cabinet was marketed in 1923 by a small Detroit company called Nizer. The cabinets had wells for cans that would hold ice cream to keep it from melting. Ice cream vendors would reach down into the cabinet, dip into the cans, and scoop out the ice cream. A refrigeration system cooled the cabinet. The system relied on alcohol-based antifreeze, but this was replaced by salt brine, which experts thought was a safer alternative. Kelvinator bought Nizer in 1926.

Wales—fought to introduce competitive products. By 1920, the market had more than 200 models.[5] And by 1921, manufacturers were putting out more than 5,000 mechanical refrigerators in the United States each year.[6] Kelvinator captured market share with the first refrigerator to have automatic temperature control and captured 80 percent of the market by 1923.[7] Frigidaire responded by cutting its prices in half.

As the economy improved during the Roaring Twenties, so did the demand for refrigerators. And their design continued to evolve. Ice cream cabinets were added to models in 1923, soda fountain equipment in 1924, and water and milk coolers in 1927. By the end of the decade, refrigerators were

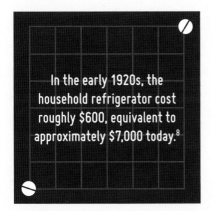

In the early 1920s, the household refrigerator cost roughly $600, equivalent to approximately $7,000 today.[8]

available in different sizes and finishes, including steel and porcelain.

A Winning Design

In 1927, Christian Steenstrup of GE designed the first all-steel refrigerator with a completely sealed refrigerating compressor system mounted in a circular unit on top. Called the Monitor Top, reportedly because it resembled the steel-clad USS *Monitor*, a battleship used during the Civil War, the refrigerator offered 14 cubic feet (0.4 cu m) of space and was among the first to rely on electricity, which had come to the majority of urban households. At $525, it was almost half the price of competitive models; by the late 1920s, the least expensive model cost $205.[9]

HEAT THAT FREEZES

Don't throw food away!

Household expenses are less in the home in which there is an "Electrolux" Refrigerator. For one thing, food never has to be thrown away because it has "gone off." Perishables like fish, meat, milk and cream can be kept fresh for days, even in thundery weather. It is a positive fact that many things, such as salads and fruit, taste better after being kept in

An English magazine advertises the Electrolux refrigerator in the 1930s.

Fueled by a $1 million advertising campaign, the Monitor Top secured GE's place as the market leader.

Although electricity was becoming standard in the United States and other industrialized countries, several manufacturers also built models to cater to rural areas that did not yet have the new mode of power. The most popular of these was the Electrolux, which was first introduced in Sweden in 1925. The Electrolux was powered by gas and used an absorption refrigeration system.

By the end of the decade, Americans had bought more than 1 million refrigerators.[10] The refrigerator now rivaled the oven as the most important and most widely used kitchen appliance.

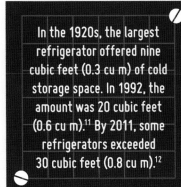

In the 1920s, the largest refrigerator offered nine cubic feet (0.3 cu m) of cold storage space. In 1992, the amount was 20 cubic feet (0.6 cu m).[11] By 2011, some refrigerators exceeded 30 cubic feet (0.8 cu m).[12]

Workers at an Electrolux factory in England put cooling units in refrigerators in 1932.

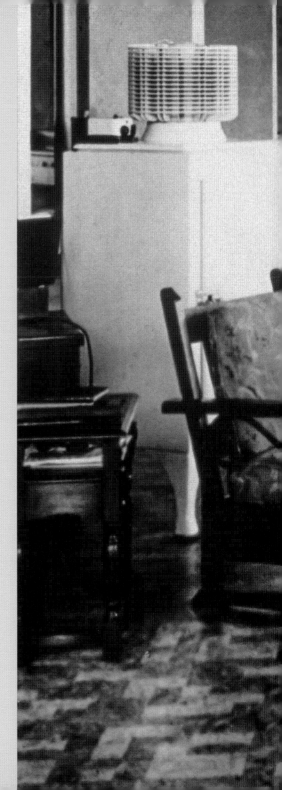

CHAPTER 7

THE FRIDGE COMES OF AGE

When electric refrigerators became available in the 1920s, they met with opposition from the established ice industry, just as Gorrie had faced when he introduced his refrigeration machine 50 years earlier. Ice harvesters and artificial ice producers joined forces as the Household Refrigeration Bureau (HRB) to spread the word about the advantages of iceboxes. The HRB argued that iceboxes did a better job of keeping food cool, saved on the cost of electricity and repairs, and were far safer than the newfangled refrigerators.

A refrigerator salesman makes his pitch to a potential customer in the 1920s.

While some consumers worried about the inconvenience of refrigerators, others worried about safety. Even as refrigerators made their way into US households in the 1910s and 1920s, many people worried about whether eating refrigerated food was safe. Concerns about safety were reinforced when people became sick from the refrigerants themselves. Refrigerators built before 1929 used methyl chloride, methyl formate, ammonia, and sulfur dioxide—chemicals that were toxic to some degree. The gases sometimes leaked from the refrigerators, causing sickness and sometimes even death. A panel of pathologists and chemists found the refrigerant methyl chloride to blame for at least 15 deaths in Chicago in 1929.[1] This resulted in a local ban on the use of the refrigerant. Such danger dissuaded consumers from buying refrigerators, and some people who owned refrigerators moved them to their backyard or another place where people would not breathe in toxic fumes if the refrigerator leaked.

Scientists and inventors looked for ways to detect leaks. In 1928, Charles Kettering, the head of research at GM, which owned Frigidaire, had asked Thomas Midgley Jr., a mechanical engineer, to find a nonflammable and nontoxic refrigerant. In 1929, Midgley and Kettering introduced their solution: dichlorodifluoromethane (CCl_2F_2), a chlorofluorocarbon (CFC) they brought to market as the product Freon. A CFC refrigerant has chlorine, fluorine, and carbon as part of its structure.

THOMAS MIDGLEY

Thomas Midgley Jr., who is credited with inventing Freon, experimented with other materials. For instance, he found a way to salt popcorn before popping. His best-known invention was "no-knock" leaded gasoline. Prior to Midgley's invention, the pistons in a car's engine often fired noisily. Midgley believed adding another chemical might cause gasoline to absorb more heat more quickly and knock less. After systematically working through the periodic table to find an appropriate additive, he found a solution in tetraethyl lead. To prove leaded gasoline was safe, Midgley once sniffed it from a flask and poured it on his hands during a press conference. This actually proved the opposite——Midgley contracted lead poisoning that would haunt him for the rest of his life. Although the federal government temporarily suspended the production of leaded gasoline in 1925, it was not until the 1970s that enough conclusive evidence came to light to force the industry to phase out leaded gasoline. Leaded gas was banned completely in the United States after 1995.

Freon: The Miracle Refrigerant

Freon, an odorless refrigerant that is not toxic to humans, became standard in refrigerators sold after 1929. In 1930, GM and DuPont, one of the world's largest chemical companies, formed the Kinetic Chemical Company to produce Freon. In a few years, compressor refrigerators using Freon became standard appliances in home kitchens. The invention of synthetic refrigerants based mostly on a CFC chemical resulted in safer refrigerators. In addition, a closely related CFC compound became widely used in air conditioning. Researchers would not realize until decades later the damage Freon caused in the environment.

The discovery of Freon removed the last obstacle to widespread adoption of refrigerators. In addition to being safer than previous refrigerants, it also needed less pressure than ammonia to vaporize at a given temperature, which made smaller and lighter machines possible. Naturally, the economic downturn during the Great Depression slowed widespread adoption of the refrigerator. By 1940, less than half of US households owned a refrigerator. The rising affluence and suburbanization following World War II contributed to making the refrigerator a mainstay of American kitchens.

The refrigerator appliance continued changing. Refrigerators became more elaborate, and companies marketed them not only as a modern convenience but also as a source of pride. Indeed, the refrigerators of the 1940s, 1950s, and 1960s came in a plethora of colors and styles, intended to match any kitchen decor.

The household refrigerator had a profound impact on the American lifestyle. Daily milk and other dairy deliveries quickly became a thing of the past. Instead of buying and eating food the same day, Americans began shopping for groceries weekly because their refrigerator would help many of their food items stay fresh longer. The refrigerator allowed owners to save time and money by buying in bulk. With the introduction of home freezers as a separate compartment and dual temperature controls in 1940, frozen foods became commonplace, making shopping, cooking, and serving healthful foods easier than ever.

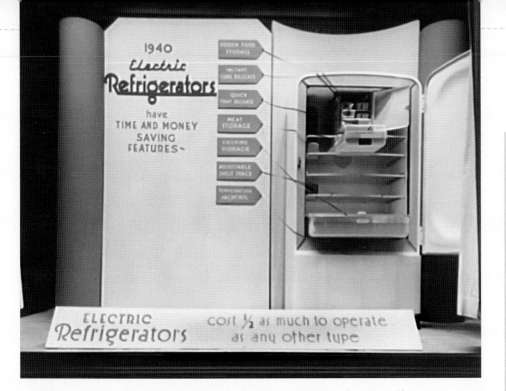

A 1940 electric refrigerator boasts many features, including a freezer with ice cube trays.

Frozen Foods

As engineers worked on improving the refrigerator, others worked on improving the foods stored in them. A young Canadian engineer named Clarence Birdseye became one of the most influential people in frozen foods.

REFRIGERATION NAMES

Because the chemical names of refrigerants can be cumbersome, DuPont developed a numbering system. DuPont originally registered the number as part of the trade name of its products. Later, the company allowed industry-wide adoption of the numbers to avoid confusion. The numbers are assigned based on their chemical makeup. Each digit within the number tells something about its atomic structure. The R at the beginning of the code stands for refrigerant. Common refrigerants have included Freon (R-12), ammonia (R-717), sulfur dioxide (R-764), and methyl chloride (R-40). Albert Henne synthesized tetrafluoroethane (R-134a) in the 1930s. It became the refrigerant of choice in the 1980s after CFCs were found to damage the ozone layer.

THE TV DINNER

With the advent of television as the main entertainment of families, the TV dinner offered the 1950s family convenience. The earliest TV dinners provided complete meals needing only to be reheated and served. Maxson Food Systems, Inc., was the first company to market a frozen meal, introducing its Strato-Plates in 1945 to airline passengers. Each Strato-Plate meal included meat, potato, and a vegetable, each housed in its own compartment. Several companies took this idea into US homes. Among the first successful companies was Frozen Dinners, Inc. Beginning in 1949, it sold three-part frozen dinners packaged on aluminum trays. There was almost instant demand for these frozen dinners. Within a year, the company had sold more than 400,000 frozen dinners.[3] TV dinners got an additional boost from Swanson, a well-known brand that consumers valued, which joined the TV-dinner market. In its advertising campaign, Swanson linked dinner to television by calling its meals TV dinners. Soon, TV dinners had become a staple of American life.

As a young man, Birdseye had learned to ice fish from the Inuit, who let the fish freeze instantly in the frigid winter air. Birdseye noticed the fish tasted much fresher than most of the frozen food that was available for purchase at the time. In 1925, he began selling frozen fish. In 1927, Birdseye received a patent for a machine that would freeze food instantly. His machine consisted of two metal plates that were frozen to –13 degrees Fahrenheit (–25°C).[2] When food was placed between the plates, it would freeze instantly, just like the fish the Inuit caught. Freezing food instantly minimizes the formation of ice crystals, which helps food taste fresh.

Clarence Birdseye's revolutionary idea took off and required workers and conveyor belts to meet consumer demand.

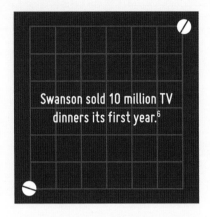

Swanson sold 10 million TV dinners its first year.[6]

In 1928, Birdseye used this flash-freezing process to introduce a line of frozen foods in addition to frozen fish—meat, fruits, and vegetables. Advertisements promised the peas were "as gloriously green as any you will see next summer."[4]

Frozen foods got a boost during World War II. Soldiers stationed overseas needed canned goods, so frozen options used fewer ration points than canned goods did. Families had a set number of ration points to use each month, so using fewer for frozen goods meant they could stretch their food budget further. Frozen foods became a staple of US grocery lists after Swanson introduced the first frozen TV dinner in 1954. The company's 1955 advertisements promised a delicious option for men looking for "a swell dinner" and convenience for women that was made possible by Swanson's "oven-ready and individual heat-and-serve trays."[5]

Refrigeration had changed home cooking. It would continue to advance and affect more than food storage and preparation.

Swanson and other companies changed the way Americans eat by providing ready-made frozen meals.

CHAPTER 8

THE FRIDGE OF THE FUTURE

Over time, refrigerators have transformed from a curiosity to a necessity. As of 2005, more than 99.9 percent of all US households had the appliance.[1] Approximately 26 percent have two or more refrigerators—a number that is growing at a rate of approximately 1 percent per year.[2] Because refrigerators take up prime real estate in the kitchen, designers have continued finding ways to improve their aesthetic appeal as well as their performance. Today's models come in a seemingly endless array of sizes, layouts, and finishes to accommodate the most finicky consumer. Ice makers have long been a standard feature for high-end refrigerators. Options let users choose between shaved, crushed, or cubed ice—often with a simple voice command. Water dispensers also

Refrigeration is popular worldwide. Japanese consumers choose among many refrigerator options just as Americans do.

REFRIGERATOR TRENDS

As of 2015, US consumers purchase more than 8 million refrigerators each year. The most popular configuration remains the top-mount refrigerator, which has a freezer on top and a refrigerator on the bottom, each with its own door. This design accounts for more than 70 percent of all refrigerator sales. The side-by-side style makes up approximately 25 percent of annual sales. The least popular model, with less than 5 percent of sales, has the freezer at the bottom of the unit, below the refrigerator.[3]

serve filtered water, seltzer water, and even hot water that can be used to make instant coffee, cocoa, or tea. On the other end of the spectrum is the HomePub, a refrigerator with a built-in system for dispensing draft beer.

Safety

One change refrigerators have undergone is related to refrigerants. Following their invention in 1929, CFCs quickly became the market-leading refrigerant. Many considered CFCs a miracle refrigerant because they were far safer for humans than ammonia, sulfur dioxide, or other substances used previously. Research undertaken in the 1970s, however, showed they were eroding the ozone layer. This upper level of the atmosphere is important to life on Earth because it

The US Environmental Protection Agency estimates, as of January 2015, 170 million refrigerators and refrigerator-freezers are currently in use in US households.[4]

KEEPING IT SAFE

Safety continues to be a refrigeration concern, but the issue regards the food inside, not the units themselves. Stashing foods in the refrigerator far longer than they should be kept, failing to maintain appropriate internal temperatures, and not thawing frozen foods properly can allow the growth of bacteria, which can cause illness. Food should not be kept past its expiration date, and it should always be kept in sealed containers. Experts advise keeping the temperature of a refrigerator between 34 degrees and 40 degrees Fahrenheit (1°C and 4°C).[5] The temperature of the freezer should never be allowed above 0 degrees Fahrenheit (–18°C).[6] To keep bacteria from building up on shelves and internal walls, a refrigerator should be cleaned routinely with soap and water. To serve as a reminder, the government has established November 15 as National Clean Out Your Fridge Day.

absorbs ultraviolet rays from the sun. Scientists warned that as a result of holes in the ozone layer, people and other living things were in danger of being exposed to ultraviolet rays that were linked to many harmful effects, including increased risk for skin cancer, danger for marine animals, and damage to crops.

The use of CFCs was among the topics discussed at an international meeting held in Montreal in 1987. In an agreement that has since become known as the Montreal Protocol, countries around the world agreed to phase out the use of CFC refrigerants. Approximately 45 countries signed the agreement in 1988. By 2009, all countries of the United Nations—more than 190—had signed the Montreal Protocol. Meanwhile, the US Congress passed the Clean Air Act of 1990, which prohibited the production of CFCs and required phasing them out by 1996. Later laws banned CFCs in new equipment beginning in 2010.

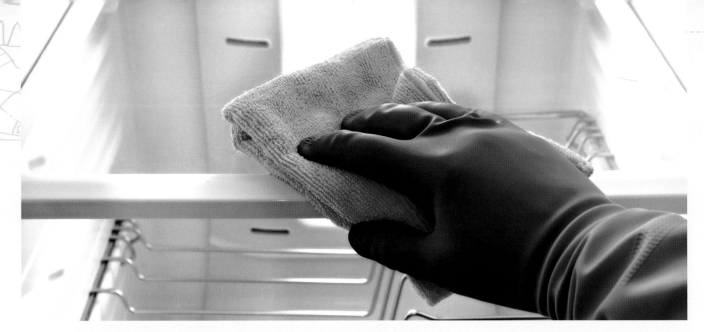

Cleaning the refrigerator helps keep bacteria at bay and limit foodborne illness.

These regulations prompted scientists to seek safer alternatives. Today, most refrigerators use hydrofluorocarbons (HFCs). Although HFCs do not cause damage to the ozone layer, environmentalists worry about their impact. The global environmental group Greenpeace maintains that the HFCs that have replaced CFCs are "super-greenhouse gases" that are exponentially more dangerous than carbon dioxide and pose an immeasurable threat to the climate.[7]

Energy Efficiency

Energy consumption is another concern about refrigerators. Unlike many other appliances, refrigerators must run continuously in order to work properly. As a result, they use more energy than other home appliances. According to the California Energy Commission, on average, refrigerators account for almost 14 percent of a household's utility costs.[8]

As government restrictions for energy efficiency have tightened in recent decades, engineers have improved efficiency via better insulation, more efficient compressors, and more precise temperature and defrost mechanisms. Despite the fact that refrigerators are, on average, 20 percent larger than they were 40 years ago, they consume less energy than those older models.[9] According to the Natural Resources Defense Council, an environmental action group, today's most energy-efficient refrigerators use less than half the energy of a model that is 12 years old.[10]

Some refrigerator designers have also focused on improving energy efficiency. Refrigerators lose cold air every time someone opens the door. See-through doors can lessen this problem. Other designs save energy with a smaller compartment for the food items used most often. The smaller space allows less air to escape and requires less energy to cool. A door-in-door refrigerator combines the two ideas by encasing food within a smaller inner door that is see-through.

ENERGY STAR

Energy Star is a voluntary program launched by the US Environmental Protection Agency in 1992. The program is designed to help businesses and individuals protect the environment by encouraging the use of energy-efficient products. Labels identify appliances that meet energy efficiency goals. The federal government has regulations regarding energy use of various appliances. For a refrigerator to receive the Energy Star rating, it must use at least 15 percent less energy than required by current federal standards.[11]

New Refrigeration Technologies

Manufacturers are experimenting in other ways, exploring new technologies to enhance energy efficiency. Some makers have built refrigerators that use solar power. These refrigerators run by means of a single, simple solar panel. Most customers who choose the solar-powered option use the refrigerators where traditional electricity is unavailable, but experts say the option is gaining popularity among environmentalists as well. The downside is, similar to anything running on solar power, they might not be the best option for parts of the country where there is not much sun.

A more practical option may be to replace the compressor with magnets. Magnetic refrigeration is not a new idea. The technology has existed since the 1880s, when Emil Warburg, a German physicist, showed that iron changed temperature when it was exposed to a changing magnetic field—a principle that became known as the magnetocaloric effect. Warburg determined some magnetic materials heat up when placed in a magnetic field and then cool down when they are removed. But the application of this discovery to refrigeration has been limited. Magnetic refrigeration systems rely on magnets that need to be cooled to extremely low temperatures. As *Newsweek* reporter Elijah Wolfson explained, "This meant giant devices—workable for big, commercial uses but useless for a window air conditioner, fridge, or really anything small enough to fit in your apartment."[12]

In March 2014, GE announced it had hit on a solution that would address the problem of size. GE's team introduced a 50-stage cooling system in which a new type of magnet lowered the temperature just a few degrees at a time. The new nickel-manganese alloy that constitutes the magnet does not need to be cooled to a ridiculously low temperature. It can function at room temperature. "Nobody in the world has done this type of multi-stage cooling," said GE researcher Venkat Venkatakrishnan.[13]

GE's development team estimates its magnetic cooling system will be 30 percent more efficient than current systems. Moreover, it will eliminate the need to produce and dispose of refrigerants. Venkatakrishnan predicts GE's magnetic cooling system will take the place of compression systems in approximately ten years. "We've spent the last 100 years to make the current refrigeration technology more efficient," explained Venkatakrishnan. "Now we are working on the technology for the next 100 years."[14]

REFRIGERATION ON THE GO

Since the refrigerator's earliest days, engineers have looked for ways to make the appliance more portable. Today, options exist for activities such as camping or fishing. Most of these refrigerators rely on absorption technology that uses ammonia as a coolant. As the ammonia moves through the appliance's cooling system, it changes from a liquid to a vapor and back again, absorbing heat from inside the refrigerator and expelling it through coils to the outside air. These refrigerators can be powered by an automobile or boat engine—some simply plug into the DC power connector. Away from electricity sources, these refrigerators can be fueled by burning gas, propane, or kerosene.

OTHER REFRIGERATION
APPLICATIONS

Refrigeration and air conditioning have much broader applications than keeping food or people cool. Cooling systems remove the heat generated by lighting, mechanical, and electric equipment. This is particularly important in computer rooms, where electronic components can overheat and fail.

In computer rooms, refrigeration balances the heat created by the popular machines.

In the manufacturing of precision metal parts, air conditioning helps maintain a uniform temperature so metals do not expand and contract. This enables precision in metalworking. Metalworkers use refrigeration to temper steel and cutlery. Tempering involves heating metal to a very high temperature and then cooling it, which ultimately makes it stronger.

Refrigeration helps metalworkers in their job.

Construction workers rely on refrigeration when working with concrete.

Hospitals store blood in refrigerators.

The construction industry uses refrigeration technologies to cool concrete. This helps keep it from cracking.

The majority of reagents—chemical substances used for laboratory testing—require refrigeration. From biotechnology labs, pharmaceutical plants, and the local pharmacy, a chain of refrigeration preserves vaccines and other medications by keeping them at consistently low temperatures.

Hospitals also rely on refrigeration to keep blood for transfusion and to preserve organs long enough to transplant them. Refrigeration helps save lives.

93

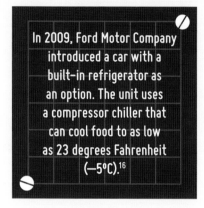

In 2009, Ford Motor Company introduced a car with a built-in refrigerator as an option. The unit uses a compressor chiller that can cool food to as low as 23 degrees Fahrenheit (—5ºC).[16]

Out of the Box

Other designers are experimenting with more radical refrigerator designs, far removed from the old-fashioned icebox. In fact, they use neither the ice nor the box. The Bio Robot, which was designed by Russian industrial design student Yuriy Dmitriev, uses a special gel that absorbs heat energy and cools through luminescence. Users insert what they want to refrigerate directly into the gel, which surrounds the food, creating separate pods for each item. In addition to providing a unique cooling solution, the design is four times smaller than conventional refrigerators and can change shape to accommodate the needs of the user. Developed for the 2010 Electrolux Design Lab competition, the Bio Robot is a design concept, not an actual product, but some people believe it may represent the future of refrigeration.

Another Electrolux Design Lab inspiration is the Impress, designed by Ben de la Roche, a student at Massey University in New Zealand, for the 2012 competition. The Impress is a customizable refrigeration wall with hexagonal cooling units de la Roche calls "pins."[15] Each pin cools individually by conduction, using sound waves in a gas-filled chamber. Food or beverages are pressed into the wall, pushing back one or more pins and activating the surrounding

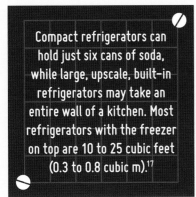

Compact refrigerators can hold just six cans of soda, while large, upscale, built-in refrigerators may take an entire wall of a kitchen. Most refrigerators with the freezer on top are 10 to 25 cubic feet (0.3 to 0.8 cubic m).[17]

pins as cooling units. De la Roche believes one of the benefits of his design is the potential energy savings. It uses less power when fewer items are pressed into it and does not refrigerate at all when empty.

Into the Future

Scientists and engineers continue making advances in refrigeration and finding new applications for refrigeration technologies. From medicine, industry, and gas and oil refineries to household kitchens, refrigeration has become a critical element of our world today.

Given the huge market for refrigerators, appliance companies will continue looking for new ways to improve on the technology and differentiate themselves from their competitors. This will no doubt result in refrigerators that are more convenient and offer better energy efficiency. What is less clear is whether tomorrow's refrigerators will continue

THE POCKET FRIDGE

While most refrigerators have gotten larger, some designers have focused on designing a portable refrigerator. In 2004, New Zealand—born designers Olaf and Uwe Diegel designed the original prototype for the Novo-Fridge. Planned for people with diabetes who need to carry insulin on the go, the pocket-size fridge can be used for any medication that has to be kept cold. The fridge, which is battery operated and can be recharged at night, is available from MedActiv, the company the Diegel brothers formed to sell their product.

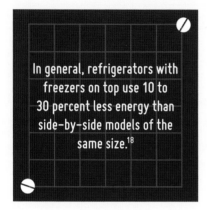

In general, refrigerators with freezers on top use 10 to 30 percent less energy than side-by-side models of the same size.[18]

to be cooled by vapor-compression systems or whether newer technologies will change the very principles on which modern appliances are cooled. What is certain, however, is the creations that emerge will be possible because of the dedication and ingenuity of Cullen, Gorrie, Evans, and the numerous other inventors who helped develop and expand refrigeration, making a cool idea into cool reality.

More than keeping food cool, refrigerators today serve as family art galleries and message centers.

THE NEXT
GENERATION: THE SMART FRIDGE

Appliance manufacturers are creating "smart" refrigerators that do far more than keep food cold. Some have built-in touch screens that keep track of the food in the refrigerator. The appliances use this information to offer meal and recipe suggestions based on what is available. The smartest refrigerators can also plan the menu around customized profiles that include likes, dislikes, and dietary restrictions. One Chinese manufacturer has included an app that automatically counts calories. Manufacturers are exploring technologies that would keep track of expiration dates and move food that is about to expire to the front of the fridge, where it is less likely to be forgotten. Others envision the refrigerator as part of a "smart kitchen" in which the fridge will turn on the oven to the temperature required by the recommended recipe.

A women uses a touch pad on a refrigerator with Internet access.

Most smart appliances have built-in touch screens that can run apps and communicate to the outside world. This allows owners who are at the supermarket to check inventory at home using a smartphone. The smart fridge may automatically pass on the grocery list to the owner's phone or a grocery delivery service. Experts claim, in the not-too-distant future, the smart refrigerator will be a part of an integrated system that will have a

Some of today's refrigerators use smartphones to communicate with manufacturers and resolve problems without an in-home visit for service.

single user interface for all appliances and the food pantry as well.

The main goal of smart appliances is to save time and money. A part of LG's newest line of refrigerators is a feature called Smart Diagnosis. If something is wrong with the appliance, the owner calls the customer service department and holds his or her smartphone up to a speaker on the refrigerator that will give the diagnostic code. For a small problem, the owner receives directions on how to fix it. Larger problems are automatically reported to the repair department. The person coming to repair the unit has information about the problem and will bring the parts needed to fix the fridge rather than assessing the situation, ordering parts, and making a return visit to install the new parts.

ESSENTIAL FACTS

DATE OF INVENTION

1850: John Gorrie introduces the first practical refrigerator.

KEY PLAYERS

▶ William Cullen, a Scottish scientist, demonstrates how the rapid heating of a liquid to a gas can result in cooling, the principle behind artificial refrigeration.

▶ Thomas Moore, an American businessman and inventor, creates what he calls a "refrigerator," an icebox to cool dairy products in transport.

▶ John Gorrie, a doctor living in Florida, experiments with systems to artificially cool the air for his patients, resulting in the first practical refrigerator.

▶ James Harrison, a Scottish engineer living in Australia, installs the first refrigeration machine in a brewery.

▶ Carl von Linde, a German engineer, builds the first practical and portable compressor refrigeration machine and manufactures and markets his refrigerators.

KEY TECHNOLOGIES

▶ The earliest methods of refrigeration relied on evaporation of water at night.

▶ Vapor-compression systems circulate a liquid refrigerant that is rapidly heated to become a gas, transferring heat through evaporation and producing a cooling effect in the surroundings, followed by compression of the vapor back to its liquid form.

▶ Absorption refrigeration is a process in which heat is used to cool through the use of two fluids to remove heat through evaporation.

▶ Magnetic refrigeration is based on the magnetocaloric effect in which certain materials heat up in the presence of a magnetic field and cool in its absence.

EVOLUTION AND UPGRADES

Since William Cullen first demonstrated cooling through artificial means was possible, scientists and engineers have worked on finding practical applications. Early artificial refrigeration systems were huge machines installed in breweries and meatpacking plants. Engineers adapted the technology to make ice, enabling people to purchase artificial ice rather than natural ice for their iceboxes. Meanwhile, researchers began figuring out how to incorporate vapor compression and other refrigeration technologies into the icebox itself, giving way to the modern-day refrigerator in which the refrigeration technology is integrated into a sealed, insulated container.

IMPACT ON SOCIETY

Over time, refrigerators have become cheaper and more energy efficient. Refrigeration has become an integral part of the transportation industry. Refrigerated shipping, rail, and trucking have established a continuous cold chain that preserves food and has fundamentally changed the way people cook, eat, and live. And the development of air conditioning made many environments more comfortable, from movie theaters to airplanes to the hot desert, where cities have bloomed.

QUOTE

"Refrigeration brought distant production centers and the North American population together. It tore down the barriers of climates and seasons. And while it helped to rev up industrial processes, it became an industry itself."

—*Barbara Krasner-Khait*, History Magazine, *Feb./Mar. 2000*

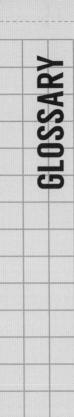

GLOSSARY

centrifugal
Moving away from the center.

chlorofluorocarbon (CFC)
Any of a class of compounds of chlorine, fluorine, and carbon, typically used in refrigeration and aerosols.

closed loop
A type of system in which the complete path is internal so the output is returned to become the input.

compressor
The pump within a refrigeration system that builds up and maintains pressure to cause the refrigerant to condense at a higher temperature, evaporate at a lower temperature, and maintain continuous flow through the system.

evaporative cooling
A process that cools the air through the evaporation of water; also called a swamp cooler.

humidity
The amount of moisture in the air or within a system.

icebox
A cabinet that uses ice as a coolant.

insulation
Any material that blocks the transfer of heat.

mechanical refrigeration
The removal of heat with a machine to produce ice or temperatures that are cooler than the surrounding temperatures.

patent

A permit issued by a government that grants a person the legal right to use or market an invention, technology, or process.

physiological chemistry

A branch of science that deals with the chemical aspects of biological systems.

refrigerant

A substance, usually liquid, used to provide cooling as the working substance of an electricity-driven vapor-compression refrigeration system or a heat-operated vapor-absorption system.

refrigeration

A process by which heat is removed or transferred, resulting in cooling air or other substances below the ambient, or surrounding, temperature in an enclosed system.

refrigeration system

Any closed-loop system that uses vapor compression or absorption to remove heat and cause cooling.

vapor compression

A type of refrigeration in which a compressor causes cooling by changing a refrigerant from a liquid to a gas and back.

ADDITIONAL RESOURCES

SELECTED BIBLIOGRAPHY

Basile, Salvatore. *Cool: How Air Conditioning Changed Everything*. New York: Fordham UP, 2014. Print.

Freidberg, Susanne. *Fresh: A Perishable History*. Cambridge, MA: Belknap, 2009. Print.

Krasner-Khait, Barbara. "The Impact of Refrigeration." *History Magazine*. Moorshead Magazines, Feb./Mar. Web. 25 Jan. 2015.

Morris, Elli. "Making Ice in Mississippi," *Mississippi History Now*. Mississippi Historical Society, May 2010. Web. 25 Jan. 2015.

Schultz, Eric B. *Carrier: Weathermakers to the World*. Gaithersburg, MD: Carrier Corporation, 2012. Print.

Weightman, Gavin. *The Frozen Water Trade: A True Story*. New York: Hyperion, 2003. Print.

FURTHER READINGS

Marling, Karal Ann. *Ice: Great Moments in the History of Hard, Cold Water*. Saint Paul, MN: Borealis, 2008. Print.

100 Inventions That Made History. New York: DK Publishing, 2014. Print.

Pringle, Laurence. *Ice! The Amazing History of the Ice Business*. Honesdale, PA: Calkins Creek, 2012. Print.

Rees, Jonathan. *Refrigeration Nation: A History of Ice, Appliances, and Enterprise in America*. Baltimore, MD: Johns Hopkins UP, 2013. Print.

WEBSITES

To learn more about Essential Library of Inventions, visit **booklinks.abdopublishing.com**. These links are routinely monitored and updated to provide the most current information available.

FOR MORE INFORMATION

For more information on this subject, contact or visit the following organizations:

John Gorrie Museum State Park

3900 Commonwealth Boulevard
Tallahassee, FL 32399
850-245-2157
http://www.floridastateparks.org/park/John-Gorrie-Museum

Learn about John Gorrie and see a model of his ice-making machine.

Refrigeration Research Museum

Two Park Avenue
New York, NY 10016-5990
800-843-2763
http://www.asme.org

Explore the American Society of Mechanical Engineers' collection showing many of the advances in mechanical refrigeration for US residential and commercial use from 1890 to 1960.

Western Pacific Railroad Museum

700 Western Pacific Way
Portola, CA 96122
530-832-4131
http://www.wplives.org

This museum has one of the most complete collections of reefers, or refrigerator cars, of any museum in the country.

SOURCE NOTES

Chapter 1. A Cool Miracle

1. Minna Scherlinder Morse. "Chilly Reception." *Smithsonian Magazine*. Smithsonian, July 2002. Web. 23 Mar. 2015.

2. George L. Chapel. "Dr. John Gorrie: Refrigeration Pioneer." *University of Florida Department of Physics*. University of Florida Department of Physics, n.d. Web. 23 Mar. 2015.

3. "Scottish Fact of the Day: William Cullen: Inventor of Refrigeration," *Scotsman*. Johnston Publishing, 30 Jan. 2013. Web. 23 Mar. 2015.

4. "Gorrie Ice Machine, Patent Model." *National Museum of American History*. Smithsonian, n.d. Web. 23 Mar. 2013.

5. "Famous Floridians: Dr. John Gorrie." *Exploring Florida*. Florida Center for Instructional Technology, 2002. Web. 23 Mar. 2015.

6. Minna Scherlinder Morse. "Chilly Reception." *Smithsonian Magazine*. Smithsonian, July 2002. Web. 23 Mar. 2015.

7. "Household Refrigerators and Home and Farm Freezers." *Highbeam Business*. Cengage, 2015. 23 Mar. 2015.

Chapter 2. Before the Fridge

1. Barbara Krasner-Khait. "The Impact of Refrigeration." *History Magazine*. History Magazine, Feb./Mar. 2000. Web. 23 Mar. 2015.

2. Ibid.

3. Daniel Calandro. "Hudson River Valley Icehouses and Ice Industry." *Hudson River Valley Institute*. Hudson River Valley Institute, 9 May 2005. Web. 23 Mar. 2015.

4. Philip Chadwick Foster Smith. "Crystal Blocks of Yankee Coldness." *Ice Harvesting USA*. NP, n.d. Web. 23 Mar. 2015.

5. Shirley Tempel Fulton. "Fond Memories: Northern Sullivan County, New York, Its History and Lore." *Catskill*. Purple Mountain Press, 2007. Web. 23 Mar. 2015.

6. Barbara Krasner-Khait. "The Impact of Refrigeration." *History Magazine*. History Magazine, Feb./Mar. 2000. Web. 23 Mar. 2015.

7. Bodil Bjerkvik Blain. "Melting Markets: The Rise and Decline of the Anglo-Norwegian Ice Trade, 1850–1920." *London School of Economics*. London School of Economics, 2006. Web. 23 Mar. 2015.

8. "Lesson 1: History of Refrigeration." *NPTEL*. Indian Institute of Technology, 2006. Web. 23 Mar. 2015.

Chapter 3. Forerunners to the Fridge

1. David Banks. *An Introduction to Thermogeology: Ground Source Heating and Cooling*. New York: Wiley, 2012. Print. Section 5.3.

2. Elli Morris. "Making Ice in Mississippi." *Mississippi History Now*. Mississippi Historical Society, May 2010. Web. 23 Mar. 2015.

3. Ibid.

4. H. J. Kreuzer and Isaac Tamblyn. *Thermodynamics*. Singapore: World Scientific, 2010. 113. *Google Books*. Web. 23 Mar. 2015.

5. Elli Morris. "Making Ice in Mississippi." *Mississippi History Now*. Mississippi Historical Society, May 2010. Web. 23 Mar. 2015.

Chapter 4. Refrigerated Transport

1. *The Strawberry*. Three Rivers, MI: Kellogg Publishing, Jan. 1906. *Internet Archive*. Web. 23 Mar. 2015.

2. Linda Danes-Wingett. "The Ice Car Cometh: A History of the Railroad Refrigerator Car." *San Joaquin Historian*. San Juan Historical Society and Museum, winter 1996. Web. 23 Mar. 2015.

3. Patents. "Improved Refrigerator-Car: US 71423 A." *Google*. Web. 23 Mar. 2015.

4. "November 26—Today in Food History." *FoodReference.com*. James T. Ehler and FoodReference.com, 2015. Web. 23 Mar. 2015.

5. Susanne Freidberg. *Fresh: A Perishable History*. Cambridge, MA: Belknap, 2009. Print. 67.

6. Ibid. 72.

7. Janet Clarkson. *Food History Almanac: Over 1,300 Years of World Culinary History, Culture, and Social Influence*. Lanham, MD: Rowman & Littlefield, 2014. Print. 493.

8. Barbara Krasner-Khait. "The Impact of Refrigeration." *History Magazine*. History Magazine, Feb./Mar. 2000. Web. 23 Mar. 2015.

9. Susanne Freidberg. *Fresh: A Perishable History*. Cambridge, MA: Belknap, 2009. Print. 47.

Chapter 5. Air Conditioning Is Born

1. "Willis Carrier." *Carrier*. Carrier Corporation, 2015. Web. 23 Mar. 2015.

2. "The Launch of Carrier Air Conditioning Company." *Willis Carrier*. United Technologies Corporation, 2015. Web. 23 Mar. 2015.

3. "The Invention That Changed the World." *Willis Carrier*. United Technologies Corporation, 2015. Web. 23 Mar. 2015.

4. Ibid.

5. "Air Conditioning and Refrigeration History." *Greatest Achievements*. National Academy of Engineering, 2015. Web. 23 Mar. 2015.

6. "Carrier Unveils Innovative Solution to Preserve Michelangelo's Frescoes in the Sistine Chapel." *Carrier*. Carrier Corporation, 29 Oct. 2014. Web. 23 Mar. 2015.

7. "Air Conditioning and Refrigeration Timeline." *Great Achievements*. National Academy of Engineering, 2015. Web. 23 Mar. 2015.

8. Ibid.

9. Ibid.

10. Rebecca J. Rosen. "Keepin' It Cool: How the Air Conditioner Made Modern America." *Atlantic*. Atlantic Monthly Group, 14 July 2011. Web. 23 Mar. 2015.

Chapter 6. The Fridge Comes Home

1. Susanne Freidberg. *Fresh: A Perishable History.* Cambridge, MA: Belknap, 2009. Print. 38.

2. "Remembering 12 Chicago Firefighters." *Honoring Heroes.* Honoring Heroes, 2011. Web. 23 Mar. 2015.

3. Carroll Gantz. "G.E. Monitor Top Refrigerator." *IndustrialDesignHistory.com.* n.p, 14 Apr. 2010. Web. 23 Mar. 2015.

4. Lindsey Chapman. "The History of the Refrigerator: Staying Cool throughout the Ages." *Finding Dulcinea.* Dulcinea, 24 Nov. 2010. Web. 24 Feb. 2010.

5. "The Story of the Refrigerator." *Association of Home Appliance Manufacturers.* Association of Home Appliance Manufacturers, n.d. Web. 23 Mar. 2015.

6. Barbara Krasner-Khait. "The Impact of Refrigeration." *History Magazine.* History Magazine, Feb./Mar. 2000. Web. 23 Mar. 2015.

7. "Air Conditioning and Refrigeration History— Part 3." *Greatest Achievements.* National Academy of Engineering, 2015. Web. 23 Mar. 2015.

8. Edward Tenner. "The Refrigerator's Cool Century." *American.* American Enterprise Institute, 3 July 2014. Web. 23 Mar. 2015.

9. "The Iceman Goeth Away: GE Monitor Tops." *Sears Modern Homes.* Sears Modern Homes, 14 May 2012. Web. 23 Mar. 2015.

10. Barbara Krasner-Khait. "The Impact of Refrigeration." *History Magazine.* History Magazine, Feb./Mar. 2000. Web. 23 Mar. 2015.

11. "Refrigerator Guide." *Inside Advantage.* Whirlpool Corporation, 2015. Web. 23 Mar. 2015.

12. "Here It Is, the Biggest Refrigerator We've Ever Tested." *Consumer Reports.* Consumer Reports, 26 Oct. 2011. Web. 18 Feb. 2015.

Chapter 7. The Fridge Comes of Age

1. Carmen J. Giunta. "Thomas Midgley Jr., and the Invention of Chlorofluorocarbon Refrigerants: It Ain't Necessarily So." *Bulletin of the History of Chemistry.* 31.2 (2006): 67. University of Illinois at Urbana-Champaign School of Chemical Sciences, n.d. Web. 23 Mar. 2015.

2. "The Strange History of Frozen Food: From Clarence Birdseye to the Distinguished Order of Zerocats." *Eater.* Vox Media, 21 Aug. 2014. Web. 23 Mar. 2015.

3. "Who 'Invented' the TV Dinner?" *Everyday Mysteries.* Library of Congress, 23 Aug. 2010. Web. 23 Mar. 2015.

4. "The Strange History of Frozen Food: From Clarence Birdseye to the Distinguished Order of Zerocats." *Eater.* Vox Media, 21 Aug. 2014. Web. 23 Mar. 2015.

5. "Vintage 1955 Swanson TV Dinner Commercial," *YouTube.* YouTube, 7 Mar. 2013. Web. 23 Mar. 2015.

6. "The Strange History of Frozen Food: From Clarence Birdseye to the Distinguished Order of Zerocats." *Eater.* Vox Media, 21 Aug. 2014. Web. 23 Mar. 2015.

Chapter 8. The Fridge of the Future

1. Robert Rector and Rachel Sheffield. "Air Conditioning, Cable TV, and an Xbox: What Is Poverty in the United States Today?" *Heritage Foundation*. Heritage Foundation, 19 July 2011. Web. 23 Mar. 2015.

2. Chris Mooney. "Why It's Not Okay to Have a Second Refrigerator." *Washington Post*. Washington Post, 26 Nov. 2014. Web. 23 Mar. 2014.

3. "Food Storage/Cooking: For Your Home." *Energy Guide*. Aclara Technologies, 2015. Web. 23 Mar. 2015.

4. "Refrigerators for Consumers." *Energy Star*. Energy Star, n.d. Web. 23 Mar. 2015.

5. "Storage Tips for Fresh Fruits and Vegetables." *Samaritan Health Services*. Samaritan Health Services, 6 Aug. 2010. Web. 23 Mar. 2015.

6. "Are You Storing Food Safely?" *FDA*. US Food and Drug Administration, 20 Jan. 2015. Web. 23 Mar. 2015.

7. "HFCs: A Growing Threat to the Climate: The Worst Greenhouse Gases You've Never Heard of . . ." *Greenpeace*. Greenpeace International, 2009. Web. 23 Mar. 2015.

8. "Refrigerators and Freezers." *Consumer Energy Center*. California Energy Commission, 2015. Web. 23 Mar. 2015.

9. "New Refrigerator Standards the 'Coolest Yet.'" *Alliance to Save Energy*. Alliance to Save Energy, 26 Aug. 2011. Web. 23 Mar. 2015.

10. "Efficient Appliances Save Energy—and Money." *Natural Resources Defense Council*. Natural Resources Defense Council, 13 Jan. 2010. Web. 23 Mar. 2013.

11. "Energy Star Qualified Appliances: Save Energy through Advanced Technologies." *Energy Star*. United States Environmental Protection Agency, n.d. Web. 24 Mar. 2014.

12. Elijah Wolfson. "Magnetic Cooling Will Put Your Refrigerator to Shame." *Newsweek*. Newsweek, 19 June 2014. Web. 23 Mar. 2015.

13. Darren Quick. "Your Next Fridge Could Keep Cold More Efficiently Using Magnets." *Gizmag*. Gizmag, 13 Feb. 2014. Web. 23 Mar. 2015.

14. Ibid.

15. "Refrigerators and Freezers." *Consumer Energy Center*. California Energy Commission, 2015. Web. 23 Mar. 2015.

16. Sarah A. Webster. "Real Fridge, Real Cool." *FordOnline*. Ford Motor Company, 22 May 2008. Web. 23 Mar. 2015.

17. Karie Lapham Fay. "Dimensions of a Standard Size Refrigerator." *SFGate*. Hearst Communications, 2015. Web. 23 Mar. 2015.

18. "Refrigerators and Freezers." *Consumer Energy Center*. California Energy Commission, 2015. Web. 23 Mar. 2015.

INDEX

agricultural specialization, 50
air conditioning, 8, 18, 19, 42,
    54, 58–62, 77, 90, 92
    cooling rooms and
        buildings, 58
    population shift, 61–62
    public transportation, 60
    shopping, 60
American Civil War, 35, 71
artificial ice rinks, 35

Bacon, Francis, 23
Birdseye, Clarence, 79, 81–82

Carré, Ferdinand, 34–35
Carrier, Willis, 54, 57, 59–61, 62
Carrier Corporation, 59
Chase, Andrew, 47, 49
Clean Air Act, 87
cold-storage warehouses,
    38, 41
Cramer, Stuart H., 59, 60
crisper, 68
Cullen, William, 12, 19, 96

Davidson, William Soltau,
    50–51
disease, 8, 14, 26, 48, 49–50
Domelre, 19, 68–69
Dunedin, 51

Earle, Parker, 44
energy efficiency, 88–89, 90, 95
Energy Star, 89
Evans, Oliver, 12–13, 96
evaporative cooling, 59

fishing, 37, 91
food poisoning, 20
Ford Motor Company, 94
freezer, 78, 86, 87, 95, 96
Freon, 76–78, 79
Frigidaire, 69, 70, 76
frozen foods, 78–79, 81–82, 87

General Electric, 19, 67, 69
General Motors, 69, 76–77
Gorrie, John, 6, 8, 10, 12, 14, 16,
    18, 19, 32, 54, 74, 96
Great Depression, 78
Guardian Refrigerator, 68–69

Harrison, James, 19, 32, 50
Henne, Albert, 79
Household Refrigeration
    Bureau, 74
humidity, 57, 59–60, 68

ice cream cabinet, 70
ice cube tray, 8
ice delivery, 27–28, 38
ice harvesting, 16, 23–26, 28,
    30, 35–37, 44, 74
ice plants, 35–37, 38, 64
icebox, 16, 19, 26–28, 38, 64, 67,
    68, 74, 94
intercontinental shipping,
    50–52

Kelvinator, 69–70
Kettering, Charles, 76

Ladies' Home Journal, 52
lifestyle changes, 78
Linde, Carle von, 19, 38, 39,

About the Author

Lydia Bjornlund is a freelance writer and editor. She has written more than two dozen nonfiction books for children and teens, mostly on American history and health-related topics. She also writes a wide variety of educational materials, including curriculum, lesson plans, textbooks, and assessment items. Bjornlund holds a master's degree in education from Harvard University and a bachelor's degree in American studies from Williams College. She lives in Virginia with her husband, Gerry Hoetmer, and their children, Jake and Sophia.